Papatango Theatre Compan~ ~ ~~~~~~hip with
Neil McPherson for the Finb

The World Premiere of

C000185916

PACK

by Louise Monaghan

PAPAtango

FINBOROUGH | THEATRE

First performance at the Finborough Theatre: Tuesday, 27 November 2012

PACK
by Louise Monaghan

Cast in order of appearance

Deb	**Angela Lonsdale**
Stephie	**Sarah Smart**
Dianna	**Denise Black**
Nasreen	**Amita Dhiri**

Director	**Louise Hill**
Designer	**Olivia Altaras**
Costume Designer	**Sarah Vigars**
Lighting Designer	**Neill Brinkworth**
Composer	**Craig Adams**
Sound Designer	**Paul Gavin**
Production Manager	**Jane Arnold-Forster**
Stage Manager	**Roisin Symes**
Casting Director	**Lucy Casson**
Vocal Coach	**Patricia Logue**
Associate Lighting Designer	**Miguel Vicente**
Assistant Stage Manager	**Judy Liao**
Producer	**Chris Foxon**

The action takes place in Leeds, present day.

The performance lasts approximately 90 minutes.

There will be no interval.

Cast and Creative Team

Denise Black | Dianna
Theatre includes *Sister Act* (national tour); *Calendar Girls* (national tour); *Mrs Warren's Profession, Yerma, Roots* (Royal Exchange Theatre, Manchester); *Who's Afraid of Virginia Woolf* (Liverpool Playhouse); *The Seagull* (Royal Court Theatre); *Sisters* (Sheffield Crucible); *Bedroom Farce* (West Yorkshire Playhouse); *The Mistress* (Sherman Cymru); *Aristo* (Chichester Festival Theatre). Television includes *Queer as Folk, Coronation Street, Small Island, Doc Martin, Robin Hood, Casualty, New Tricks, The Bill, No Angels, Born and Bred, Doctors, Holby City, Midsomer Murders, The Brief, Viva Las Blackpool, Clocking Off, The Vice, The Scarlet Pimpernel, Bad Girls, Sins, Things You Do For Love, Macbeth.* Film includes *Joy Rider, Last Orders.*

Amita Dhiri | Nasreen
Theatre includes *After the Gods* (Hampstead Theatre); *Feelgood* (Hampstead Theatre/ Garrick Theatre); *The Crucible* (Leicester Haymarket Theatre); *Whose Life Is It Anyway* (Comedy Theatre). Television includes *The Bill, Holby City, Judge John Deed, Silent Witness, Second Generation, Being April, Dalziel and Pascoe, The Law, Grease Monkeys, This Life.* Film includes *Acts of God, 24 Hours in London.* Radio includes *Skios* by Michael Frayn.

Angela Lonsdale | Deb
Trained at the RSAMD. Theatre includes *Bluebird* (Royal Court Theatre); *Black and White Shorts* (Paines Plough); *Gertrude's Secret* (Grand Theatre, Leeds/Oxford Playhouse); *The Long Line, She Stoops to Conquer, And a Nightingale Sang* (Northern Stage); *Women in Love* (Durham Theatre Company).Television includes *Coronation Street, Joe Maddison's War, Best Possible Taste, All Quiet on the Preston Front, Finney, Kavanagh QC, Wolfblood, The Bill, The Royal, Picking Up the Pieces, City Central, Holby City, Casualty, Justice for Gemma, The Vanishing Man, A Touch of Frost, Hetty Wainthrop Investigates, Peak Practice.*

Sarah Smart | Stephie

Sarah has been acting since she was ten years old and trained at the Central Junior Television Workshop in Birmingham. Theatre includes *The Railway Children* (Birmingham Repertory Theatre); *Ghosts* (Gate Theatre); *The Line* (Arcola Theatre); *Like a Fishbone* (Bush Theatre). Television includes *The Secret of Crickley Hall*, *Wallander*, *Doctor Who*, *Funland*, *Jane Hall*, *At Home with the Braithwaites*, *Sparkhouse*, *Murder Prevention*, *Five Days*, *Midsomer Murders*, *Casualty 1906–1909*, *Poirot*, *Miss Marple*, *David Copperfield*, *Soldier Soldier*, *Monroe*, *The Man Who Crossed Hitler*, *Wuthering Heights*, *Death in Paradise*, *Fast Freddie*, *The Widow and Me* and the children's series *Woof!*. Radio includes many radio plays for BBC Radio 4.

Louise Monaghan | Playwright

Louise was the winner of a Bruntwood Prize Judges' Award 2011 for *Shadow Play*. Her first radio drama *Alone in the Garden with You*, produced and directed by Jessica Dromgoole, was broadcast on BBC Radio 4 earlier this year. In 2006, she was a member of 'The Fifty,' a new-writing initiative run by the Royal Court Theatre in conjunction with the BBC. Her other plays include *Beautiful* – nominated by Out Of Joint Theatre Company for the Susan Smith Blackburn Prize 2009, and *Aurora*, which was a finalist for both the London Festival New Writing Award and Little Brother's Big Opportunity competition 2010. She was shortlisted for Theatre Centre's Adrienne Benham Award 2012 and is a member of their Skylines group.

Louise Hill | Director

At the Finborough Theatre Louise directed *What Every Woman Knows* (2010) and *Quality Street* (2010), for which she was named Best Newcomer Director by the British Theatre Guide and nominated as Best Director at the OffWestEnd Awards, and *Outward Bound* (2012). Trained at Bristol Old Vic Theatre School and spent two years as Artistic Director of the Bristol Shakespeare Festival. Most recently, she directed David Mamet's *Boston Marriage* for Royal Welsh College of Music and Drama. Other directing includes *Spiders and Crocodile Tears* (Soho Theatre Studio); *To a Sunless Sea* (Etcetera Theatre); *Face to Face* (Old Red Lion Theatre); *The Merchant of Venice* and *The Taming of the Shrew* (Middle Temple Gardens); *Tiny Dynamite* (Alma Tavern Theatre, Bristol) and *IAGO*, her own adaptation of *Othello*, for which she won a Fringe Review Outstanding Theatre Award at the Edinburgh Festival. She was Associate Director on *Travesties* and *The Importance of Being Earnest* (Birmingham Rep). Assistant Direction includes *Blackbird* and *The Winslow Boy* (both Salisbury Playhouse).

Olivia Altaras | Designer

At the Finborough Theatre Olivia designed *S27*, *The December Man* and *Love on the Dole*. Studied History of Art and English at the University of Leeds and is currently studying a Masters in Participatory and Community Arts at Goldsmiths. Theatre as designer includes *Street Runners* (Blaze Festival); *Barbarians* (Tooting Arts Club); *The Merry Widow* (Folkwang Universität der Künst); *The Uncommercial Traveller*, *Space Invaders*, *The Night Chauffeur*, *Grey Goose Project*, *Under the Eiderdown*, *Haunted Park*, *Rose Bruford Symposium Festival* (Punchdrunk); *Gotcha*, *Fragments* (Riverside Studios); *A Moment of Silence*, *Ordinary Lads* (Etcetera Theatre). Theatre as part of the design team includes *The Duchess of Malfi* (Punchdrunk); *Gamerunners* (Roundhouse Studios) and *The Masque of the Red Death* (BAC/Punchdrunk).

Sarah Vigars | Costume Designer

Sarah trained at the Royal Welsh College of Music and Drama. Theatre includes *Arabian Nights*, *Black Sail White Sail*, *Death and the Nightingale* and *Boston Marriage* (RWCMD), and work as an associate designer for National Youth Theatre Wales's summer tour. Theatre as assistant designer includes Frantic Assembly and National Theatre Wales's *Little Dogs* (Patti Pavilion, Swansea), and *Lemony Snicket's Latke Who Couldn't Stop Screaming* (Roundhouse).

Neill Brinkworth | Lighting Designer

At the Finborough Neil was Lighting Designer on *Fair* (2005), *Accolade* (2011), *Fanta Orange* (2011), *Don Juan Comes Back From the War* (2012) and *Outward Bound* (2012). Theatre includes *In the Night Garden* (Minor/Rag Doll/BBC); *The Seagull* (Arcola Theatre); *Fair*, *Tape*, *Step 9 of 12*, *Vincent River* (Trafalgar Studios); *Agamemnon* (Cambridge Arts Theatre); *Seven Pomegranate Seeds* (Oxford Playhouse); *Deptford Stories* (National Theatre); *Six Men & A Poker Game* (Gridiron); *A Square of Sky*, *In the Store Room* (The Kosh); *Romeo and Juliet*, *Cats*, *Wedding Singer*, *Footloose* (Arts Ed); *Spangleguts*, *The Tinder Box* (London Bubble); *Blood Wedding*, *Nicholas Nickleby* (Guildhall); *The Handsomest Drowned Man* (Circus Space); *A Christmas Carol* (Southwark Playhouse). Opera includes *Dido and Aeneas*, *Jephthe* (ETO); *Bridgetower* (City of London/ETO); and, as Associate Lighting Designer, includes *Ludd and Isis* (Royal Opera House); *Maria Stuarda* (Opera North). Forthcoming productions include *The Tin Solider* (peut etre); *Dick Whittington* (Hertford); *Café Chaos* (The Kosh).

Craig Adams | Composer

Craig Adams is a composer, lyricist and arranger and is currently
Cameron Mackintosh Composer-in-Residence at the Finborough
Theatre. At the Finborough Theatre Craig's work includes *Thérèse
Raquin* (2012) and *Hindle Wakes* (2012). Theatre includes *The
Seventh Muse* (Plymouth Arts Centre); *Battlements* (Vanburgh
Theatre); *The Watchers* (Bradford Playhouse); *Ghosts of the Past*
(Aberdeen Playhouse); *LIFT* (Trafalgar Studios); *Ballet People* (The
Place); *Thérèse Raquin* (Theatre Royal, Drury Lane); *Let Him Have
Justice* (Cochrane Theatre). Musical arrangements/composition
/direction include *Kerry Ellis LIVE at the Hippodrome* and *Kerry Ellis –
The Great British Songbook* (Shaw Theatre); Julie Atherton's new
album *No Space for Air*, The Franks' new album *Love/Drunk/Soul*,
Louise Dearman's *Up Close* and the *LIFT* concept album. Craig
devised the musicals *Bed*, *Apartment 15* and *Festival*.
Craig was Musical Director on *Oh! What a Lovely War* (RADA) among
many others. Craig is currently working on a revue for ANMT, LA and
LIFT can be seen at the Soho Theatre in February 2013.
www.craigadamsmusic.com

Paul Gavin | Sound Designer

At the Finbrough Theatre Paul designed sound for *Crush* (2011) and
Through The Night (2011). Trained at RADA. Theatre includes *Sit
and Shiver*, *Face Value*, *A Mother Speaks*, *40*, *Brothers* (Hackney
Empire); *The Famous Compere's Police Dog Balls* (Duke of York
Theatre); *Lottie's Journey* (New End Theatre); *Circus of Illusions*,
The Circus of Rock and Roll, *Sweet Charity*, *Spring Awakening*,
Cinderella, *Godspell* (Blackheath Concert Halls); *Once on this Island*
(national tour). Paul designed and worked on many of the
productions at Hackney Empire Theatre between 1990 and 2010
including eight of their famous pantomimes.

Jane Arnold-Forster| Production Manager

At the Finborough Theatre, Jane was production manager on *The
Roar of the Greasepaint*, *The Smell of the Crowd* (2011), *Foxfinder*
as part of the 2011 Papatango New Writing Festival (2011), and *A
Life* (2012). Production Management includes, most recently,
Production Manager for *Ignorance/Jahiliyyah* (Hampstead Theatre);
La bohème (Charing Cross Theatre); *The Only True History of Lizzie
Finn* (Southwark Playhouse); *Brimstone and Treacle* (Arcola
Theatre); *Acante et Céphise* (Bloomsbury Theatre); *Lagan*
(Ovalhouse) and *Don Giovanni* (Soho Theatre).

Roisin Symes | Stage Manager
At the Finborough Theatre Roisin stage-managed *Rigor Mortis* (2011).
Trained at LAMDA. Theatre includes *The Madwoman Of Chaillot*
(Cockpit Theatre); *The Magpies, The Wolves* (Tristan Bates
Theatre); *Orlando* (BAC); *Many Moons* (Theatre503).

Lucy Casson | Casting Director
Lucy is currently one of the Resident Casting Directors at the
Finborough Theatre. At the Finborough Lucy cast *Through the Night*
(2011); *Rigor Mortis* (2011; as Casting Assistant); *Crush* (2011; as
Casting Assistant); *Autumn Fire* (2012); *Merrie England* (2012); *The
Fear of Breathing* (2012); *The Sluts of Sutton Drive* (2012);
Cornelius (2012). Other theatre includes *The Seagull* (Southwark
Playhouse); *The Art of Concealment* (Riverside Studios). Film
includes *Tested* and *The Dark Road* starring Con O'Neill (both as
Casting Assistant).

Miguel Vicente | Associate Lighting Designer
Trained at the London Academy of Music and Dramatic Art (LAMDA).
At the Finborough Theatre, Miguel was Lighting Designer for
Through the Night (2011); *Autumn Fire* (2012); *Merrie England*
(2012); *Barrow Hill* (2012); *Passing By* (2012); *The Fear of
Breathing* (2012). Theatre includes Laura Wade's *Other Hands*
(national tour); *Missing* (Tristan Bates Theatre); *Normal?*
(Ovalhouse and LOST Theatre); *Miss Julie* (Theatro Technis); *The
Happy Prince* (Little Angel Theatre); *Chapel Street* (Old Red Lion
Theatre). At LAMDA, Miguel was the Lighting Designer for *The Last
Days of Judas Iscariot*, *Hedda Gabler*, and *Kindertransport*.

Judy Liao| Assistant Stage Manager
Judy trained at Central Academy of Drama, China, and then took a
postgraduate degree in Film Production at the University of Bristol.
Theatre includes writing and directing *The Roof* and *Dear Miss
Hanff*, and directing *Pygmalion* (all at Central Academy of Drama,
China). As an Editor film includes *Fashion Victim*.

Chris Foxon | Producer

At the Finborough Theatre Chris produced *The Fear of Breathing* (2012) and was Assistant Producer on *Don Juan Comes Back From the War* (2012). Read English at Oxford University and trained at the Central School of Speech and Drama on an AHRC Scholarship. Productions include *Old Vic New Voices 24 Hour Plays* (Old Vic Theatre); *The Madness of George III* (Oxford Playhouse); *Grave Expectations* (Compass Theatre, St Albans South Signal Box and South Hill Park); *Looking After the Pooters* (Canal Cafe Theatre). Theatre as Assistant Producer includes *On the Threshing Floor* (Hampstead Theatre); *Endless Poem* as part of *Rio Occupation London* (BAC/People's Palace Projects/HighTide Festival Theatre), and *Mudlarks* (HighTide Festival Theatre/Theatre503/Bush Theatre).

Production Acknowledgements

With thanks to Hayley Kaimakliotis, the Workspace Group, Hannah Jenner, Patricia Logue, Oliver O'Shea and Sarah Davey-Hull

PAPAtango

Papatango was founded by Matt Roberts, George Turvey and Sam Donovan in 2007. The company's mission is to find the best and brightest new talent in the UK with an absolute commitment to bring their work to the stage. 2009 saw the launch of their first Papatango New Writing Competition, which each year has gone from strength to strength.

Following the huge success of the Papatango New Writing Festival 2011 in partnership with the Finborough Theatre, which saw unprecedented press acclaim for the sell-out production of the winning play, Dawn King's *Foxfinder*, the partnership between Papatango and one of London's leading new-writing venues, the multi-award-winning Finborough Theatre, continues...

This year's competition saw 700 entries from all over the world.

This year's judges included Con O'Neill (Actor), Dawn King (Playwright), Colin Barr (BBC Director and Producer), Tamara Harvey (Director), Blanche McIntyre (Director), Neil McPherson (Artistic Director of the Finborough Theatre), Francis Grin (Literary Manager of the Finborough Theatre) and Tanya Tillett (Literary Agent, The Rod Hall Agency).

Press on *Foxfinder*

Time Out Critics' Choice
***** Five Stars WhatsOnStage
**** Four Stars *Guardian*
**** Four Stars *Evening Standard*
**** Four Stars *Spoonfed*

Guardian Critics' Choice
**** Four Stars *Telegraph*
**** Four Stars *Independent*
**** Four Stars *Exeunt*
**** Four Stars *Time Out*

One of the *Independent*'s Top Five Plays of 2011
Nominated for the Off West End Award for 2011 for Best New Play

FINBOROUGH | THEATRE

'An even more audacious and successful programme than ever in 2012, West London's tiny, unsubsidised Finborough Theatre is one of the best in the entire world. Its programme of new writing and obscure rediscoveries remains "jaw-droppingly good".' *Time Out/The Hospital Club*

'A disproportionately valuable component of the London theatre ecology. Its programme combines new writing and revivals, in selections intelligent and audacious.' *Financial Times*

'A blazing beacon of intelligent endeavour, nurturing new writers while finding and reviving neglected curiosities from home and abroad.' *Daily Telegraph*

Founded in 1980, the multi-award-winning Finborough Theatre presents plays and music theatre, concentrated exclusively on new writing and genuine rediscoveries from the 19th and 20th centuries. The Finborough Theatre remains unfunded by any public body, and our most significant subsidy comes from the distinguished actors, directors, designers and production team who work with us for minimal remuneration. We aim to offer a stimulating and inclusive programme, appealing to theatregoers of all ages and from a broad spectrum of the population. Behind the scenes, we continue to discover and develop a new generation of theatre makers – through our vibrant Literary Team, our internship programme, our Resident Assistant Director Programme, and our partnership with the National Theatre Studio providing a bursary for Emerging Directors.

Despite remaining completely unsubsidised, the Finborough Theatre has an unparalleled track record of attracting the finest creative talent, as well as discovering new playwrights who go on to become leading voices in British theatre. Under Artistic Director Neil McPherson, it has discovered some of the UK's most exciting new playwrights including Laura Wade, James Graham, Mike Bartlett, Sarah Grochala, Jack Thorne, Simon Vinnicombe, Alexandra Wood, Al Smith, Nicholas de Jongh and Anders Lustgarten.

Artists working at the theatre in the 1980s included Clive Barker, Rory Bremner, Nica Burns, Kathy Burke, Ken Campbell, Jane Horrocks and Claire Dowie. In the 1990s, the Finborough Theatre became known for new writing including Naomi Wallace's first play *The War Boys*; Rachel Weisz in David Farr's *Neville Southall's Washbag*; four plays by Anthony Neilson including *Penetrator* and *The Censor*, both of which transferred to the Royal Court Theatre; and new plays by Richard Bean, Lucinda Coxon, David Eldridge, Tony Marchant, Mark Ravenhill and Phil Willmott. New writing development included the premieres of modern classics such as Mark Ravenhill's *Shopping and F***king*, Conor McPherson's *This Lime Tree Bower*, Naomi Wallace's *Slaughter City* and Martin McDonagh's *The Pillowman*.

Since 2000, new British plays have included Laura Wade's London debut *Young Emma*, commissioned for the Finborough Theatre; James Graham's *Albert's Boy* with Victor Spinetti; Sarah Grochala's *S27*; Peter Nichols' *Lingua Franca*, which transferred Off-Broadway; Ander Lustgarten's *A Day at the Racists*; Dawn King's *Foxfinder*; and West End transfers for Joy Wilkinson's *Fair*; Nicholas de Jongh's *Plague Over England*; and Jack Thorne's *Fanny and Faggot*. The late Miriam Karlin made her last stage appearance in *Many Roads to Paradise* in 2008. Many of the Finborough Theatre's new plays have been published and are on sale from our website.

UK premieres of foreign plays have included Brad Fraser's *Wolfboy*; Lanford Wilson's *Sympathetic Magic*; Larry Kramer's *The Destiny of Me*; Tennessee Williams' *Something Cloudy, Something Clear*; the English premiere of Robert McLellan's Scots language classic, *Jamie the Saxt*; and three West End transfers – Frank McGuinness' *Gates of Gold* with William Gaunt and John Bennett, Joe DiPietro's *F***ing Men* and Craig Higginson's *Dream of the Dog* with Dame Janet Suzman.

Rediscoveries of neglected work have included the first London revivals of Rolf Hochhuth's *Soldiers* and *The Representative*; both parts of Keith Dewhurst's *Lark Rise to Candleford*; *The Women's War*, an evening of original suffragette plays; *Etta Jenks* with Clarke Peters and Daniela Nardini; Noël Coward's first play, *The Rat Trap*; Charles Wood's *Jingo* with Susannah Harker; Emlyn Williams' *Accolade* with Aden Gillett and Graham Seed; Lennox Robinson's *Drama at Inish* with Celia Imrie and Paul O'Grady; and J.B. Priestley's *Cornelius* with Alan Cox.

Music Theatre has included the new – premieres from Grant Olding, Charles Miller, Michael John LaChuisa, Adam Guettel, Andrew Lippa and Adam Gwon's *Ordinary Days* which transferred to the West End, and the old – the UK premiere of Rodgers and Hammerstein's *State Fair* which also transferred to the West End, and the acclaimed Celebrating British Music Theatre series, reviving forgotten British musicals including *Gay's The Word* by Ivor Novello with Sophie-Louise Dann, Helena Blackman and Elizabeth Seal.

The Finborough Theatre won *The Stage* Fringe Theatre of the Year Award in 2011, won *London Theatre Reviews'* Empty Space Peter Brook Award in 2010, the Empty Space Peter Brook Award's Dan Crawford Pub Theatre Award in 2005 and 2008, the Empty Space Peter Brook Mark Marvin Award in 2004, four awards in the inaugural 2011 OffWestEnd Awards and swept the board with eight awards at the 2012 OffWestEnd Awards including Best Artistic Director and Best Director for the second year running. *Accolade* was named Best Fringe Show of 2011 by *Time Out*. It is the only unsubsidised theatre to be awarded the Pearson Playwriting Award bursary for writers Chris Lee in 2000, Laura Wade in 2005, James Graham in 2006, Al Smith in 2007, Anders Lustgarten in 2009, Simon Vinnicombe in 2010 and Dawn King in 2011. Three bursary holders (Laura Wade, James Graham and Anders Lustgarten) have also won the Catherine Johnson Award for Pearson Best Play.

www.finboroughtheatre.co.uk

FINBOROUGH | THEATRE

118 Finborough Road, London SW10 9ED
admin@finboroughtheatre.co.uk
www.finboroughtheatre.co.uk

Artistic Director | **Neil McPherson**

Resident Designer | Deputy Chief Executive | **Alex Marker**

General Manager | **Laura Fry**

Pearson Playwright-in-Residence | **Dawn King**

Playwrights-in-Residence | **Bekah Brunstetter, James Graham, Anders Lustgarten, Colleen Murphy, Simon Vinnicombe**

Associate Director | **Justin Audibert**

Cameron Mackintosh Resident Composer facilitated by Mercury Musical Developments and Musical Theatre Network UK | **Craig Adams**

Literary Manager | **Francis Grin**

Literary Associate Music Theatre | **Max Pappenheim**

Technical Manager | **Jude Malcomson**

Associate Designer | **Philip Lindley**

Marketing | **Gemma Bealing**

Resident Casting Directors | **Lucy Casson, Hayley Kaimakliotis**

Resident Assistant Directors | **Dan Pick, Jack Ryder**

(Dan Pick is on attachment from the MFA in Theatre Directing at Birkbeck, University of London.)

Resident Assistant Producer | **Luke Holbrook**

And our many interns and volunteers.

The Associate Director position is supported by the National Theatre Studio's Bursary for Emerging Directors, a partnership between the National Theatre Studio and the Finborough Theatre.

The Finborough Theatre has the support of the Pearson Playwrights' Scheme. Sponsored by Pearson PLC.

The Cameron Mackintosh Resident Composer Scheme is facilitated by Mercury Musical Developments and Musical Theatre Network UK

The Finborough Theatre is a member of the Independent Theatre Council, Musical Theatre Network UK and The Earl's Court Society www.earlscourtsociety.org.uk

Mailing

Email admin@finboroughtheatre.co.uk or give your details to our Box Office staff to join our free email list. If you would like to be sent a free season leaflet every three months, just include your postal address and postcode.

Follow Us Online

 www.facebook.com/FinboroughTheatre

www.twitter.com/finborough

Feedback

We welcome your comments, complaints and suggestions. Write to Finborough Theatre, 118 Finborough Road, London SW10 9ED or email us at admin@finboroughtheatre.co.uk

Finborough Theatre T-shirts are now on sale from the Box Office, available in Small, Medium and Large £7.00

Friends

The Finborough Theatre is a registered charity. We receive no public funding, and rely solely on the support of our audiences. Please do consider supporting us by becoming a member of our Friends of the Finborough Theatre scheme. There are four categories of Friends, each offering a wide range of benefits.

Brandon Thomas Friends – Bruce Cleave. Matthew Littleford. Sean W. Swalwell. Michael Rangos. David Day

Richard Tauber Friends – Neil Dalrymple. Richard Jackson. M. Kramer. Harry MacAuslan. Brian Smith. Mike Lewendon

William Terriss Friends – Leo and Janet Liebster. Peter Lobl. Bhags Sharma. Thurloe and Lyndhurst LLP. Jon Sedmak. Jan Topham

Smoking is not permitted in the auditorium and the use of cameras and recording equipment is strictly prohibited.

In accordance with the requirements of the Royal Borough of Kensington and Chelsea:

1. The public may leave at the end of the performance by all doors and such doors must at that time be kept open.

2. All gangways, corridors, staircases and external passageways intended for exit shall be left entirely free from obstruction whether permanent or temporary.

3. Persons shall not be permitted to stand or sit in any of the gangways intercepting the seating or to sit in any of the other gangways.

The Finborough Theatre is licensed by the Royal Borough of Kensington and Chelsea to The Steam Industry, a registered charity and a company limited by guarantee. Registered in England no. 3448268. Registered Charity no. 1071304. Registered Office: 118 Finborough Road, London SW10 9ED. The Steam Industry is under the Artistic Direction of Phil Willmott. www.philwillmott.co.uk

PACK

Louise Monaghan

Characters

STEPHIE, *thirties*
DEB, *thirties*
NASREEN, *thirties*
DIANNA, *early fifties*

The play is set in Leeds.

This text went to press before the end of rehearsals and so may differ slightly from the play as performed.

Scene One

A small function room in a community centre. On a flip chart, scrawled in green ink, is 'Welcome to Beginners' Bridge. Week Two: Bidding'. The room is set up for play, several baize-covered tables each surrounded by four chairs. The door opens slowly and DEB *pokes her head around the door. She enters with* STEPHIE *in tow.*

STEPHIE. Is this it?

DEB. Yeah.

> DEB *gazes about. She fingers one of the baize-covered tables.*

> This is it.

STEPHIE. There's no one here.

DEB. We're early.

STEPHIE. There's a bar downstairs.

DEB. Be here for seven she said.

STEPHIE. It's ten to. Let's get a quick drink in.

DEB. No.

> STEPHIE *gazes about.*

STEPHIE. Think I need the toilet.

DEB. Down the hall at the top of the stairs.

STEPHIE. You might've said.

DEB. Thought you went before we come out.

STEPHIE. I did.

DEB. Well, if you wanna go…

STEPHIE. Don't you need to?

DEB. No.

STEPHIE. I'll go then.

DEB. Okay. Fine. What?

STEPHIE. Nothing.

> STEPHIE *hovers for a moment, glances at* DEB, *then exits.*
> DEB *wanders around the room and peers at the noticeboard.*
> *Exercise classes, youth club, choir, allotment association,*
> *junior chess and details of a forthcoming BNP rally. She lifts*
> *the BNP notice to look at another notice underneath.*
> DIANNA *enters.*

DIANNA. Hello there.

> DEB *turns.*

DEB. Oh, yeah. Hi. I were just... You know. Looking at
noticeboard. Might be tempted to go to that.

DIANNA. It's a free country.

DEB. Oh no, not BNP rally. Exercise class.

DIANNA. Oh, the Pilates.

> DIANNA *beams.*

I recommend it. Marvellous for the central core.

DEB. Right. Thanks.

DIANNA. Are you joining us this evening?

DEB. Me 'un a mate, yeah.

> DIANNA *approaches* DEB, *her arm outstretched to greet*
> *her.*

DIANNA. You're very welcome. I'm Dianna.

> DEB *takes her hand. They shake.*

DEB. Deb.

DIANNA. I believe we spoke on the phone?

DEB. We... Yeah.

STEPHIE *enters. She's rooting in her bag for a lippy so doesn't immediately notice* DIANNA.

STEPHIE. Dead clean them toilets. (*Applying her lippy then dropping it back in her bag. Sniffs her hand.*) 'Un the soap were that... Hello.

DIANNA. Hello. I'm Dianna.

DIANNA *reaches out to shake hands with* STEPHIE. STEPHIE *juggles with her bag, wipes her hand on her coat, then shakes* DIANNA's *hand.*

STEPHIE. Sorry. Bit clammy, me hands. I've just... Washed 'em. Sorry.

DIANNA. Fine. (*Beams.*) And you are?

STEPHIE. Stephanie. But me mates call me Steph. Stephie. Either's fine by me. Or Stephanie. Me mam always used call me Stephanie. Whereas me grandma...

DIANNA. Stephie then.

STEPHIE. Stephie.

STEPHIE *clutches her bag.*

It's new, int it? This place.

DIANNA. About nine months.

STEPHIE. I've watched it goin' up. It's on me route in to work. Morrisons. Fits in with me family, you know.

DIANNA. Oh, the one just up the road from here.

STEPHIE. That's right. I'm not on shop floor. Staff canteen.

DIANNA *nods.*

DIANNA. Let's take a seat, shall we?

STEPHIE *and* DEB *glance about, unsure about which table to sit down at.*

Anywhere will do.

*They both make as if to sit at different tables, notice their
mistake and hover, waiting for* DIANNA*'s lead.* DIANNA
sits down at the table in between them and the girls join her.
STEPHIE *puts her bag down on the floor at her feet. She
picks it up and puts it down on the other side.*

Have either of you ever played bridge before?

DEB. Never.

STEPHIE. No.

DIANNA. Whist?

STEPHIE. Beg pardon?

DEB. Have we ever played whist?

STEPHIE. I don't think… Have we?

DEB. No.

STEPHIE. No.

DIANNA. You'll pick it up.

   STEPHIE *looks at* DEB. DEB *throws her a 'What?' look.*

STEPHIE. Thought we were playing bridge.

DIANNA. Oh, absolutely. It's just that if you've ever played
   whist it might give you a better understanding of the game.

STEPHIE. Oh.

DIANNA. But it's by no means a prerequisite.

   STEPHIE *glances at* DEB.

DEB. Be fine.

   DIANNA *picks up the pack of cards.*

DIANNA. Essentially then, bridge is a game of skill and
   chance. The skills you'll need to develop are… Memory.

   DEB *nods.*

   Tactics.

STEPHIE *nods*.

And, perhaps most important of all, communication.

STEPHIE *shoots a glance at* DEB. DEB *looks away.*
DIANNA *beams reassurance at* STEPHIE *as she starts to shuffle the cards. She glances at her watch.*

Are you local?

STEPHIE. Beeston.

DEB. But I'm local.

STEPHIE. Beeston is local. Might not be Headingley but it's... Well, it's still Leeds.

DIANNA. Of course.

DIANNA *puts the cards back on the table as* NASREEN *enters.*

Nasreen.

DIANNA *gets to her feet to greet* NASREEN.

NASREEN. Sorry. We'd an emergency at the surgery.

DIANNA. No problem at all. Welcome back.

She pulls out a chair and gestures for her to sit down.

NASREEN. Thanks.

NASREEN *sits down at the table.*

DIANNA. These ladies are joining us this evening.

DIANNA *beams at* STEPHIE *and* DEB.

NASREEN. Fantastic.

NASREEN *smiles*.

DEB. Have you played before then?

NASREEN. Not in ages. I played a bit at university. But this is great, isn't it?

DIANNA *sits back down and picks up the cards again. She shuffles.*

DIANNA. Nasreen came for the first time last week.

NASREEN. I'm useless.

DIANNA. You did very well.

NASREEN. Couldn't remember a thing.

STEPHIE. My memory's crap. A bit rubbish. Sorry.

DIANNA. Don't be. You're here to have fun.

She gives STEPHIE*'s arm a friendly squeeze.*

Let's start with an introduction. Stephie?

STEPHIE. Eh?

DIANNA. Nasreen.

NASREEN. Hi, Stephie.

STEPHIE. Oh, yeah. Hi, love. Nice to meet you.

STEPHIE reaches out to NASREEN *and they shake hands.*

DIANNA. And Deb?

DEB gestures 'Hi'.

DEB. Hi.

NASREEN nods.

NASREEN. Deb.

STEPHIE. She's just up the road from here now.

DEB. I am, yeah.

STEPHIE. The Meadows.

NASREEN. No! Really? We must be neighbours.

DEB shrugs.

DEB. Are we?

NASREEN. I live just opposite the play-park.

DEB. I've never seen you before.

NASREEN. Number fifty.

DEB. Forty-three.

DIANNA. Small world.

DEB *picks her nails*.

DEB. Yeah.

She folds her arms across her chest.

DIANNA. Nasreen's my mother's GP.

DEB. A doctor?

NASREEN. The local surgery.

DEB *nods*.

But I'm not full-time. I've got a little boy. Sanjay. He's seven.

STEPHIE. Aw, lovely. We've boys an' all. Deb?

DEB. Paul. He's fourteen.

STEPHIE. And mine's called Jack. He's the same age as your Paul, int he? Fourteen.

DIANNA. A difficult age.

DEB. Not really.

NASREEN. It can be.

DEB *throws* NASREEN *a look*.

STEPHIE. Have you got any kids?

DIANNA. 'Fraid not. Oh, excuse me one moment, would you? I just need to get you some crib sheets.

DIANNA *gets up*.

STEPHIE. Can I get a glass of water? Me throat's that dry.

DIANNA. Of course. Let me show you where the kitchen is. Deb?

DEB. Fine thanks.

DIANNA *and* STEPHIE *exit*.

Me husband's doctor were Asian. Dr Bashir Sasooli. D'you know him?

NASREEN. I'm afraid not. No.

A long pause.

When did you move in?

DEB. Week ago Friday.

A pause.

You?

NASREEN. Last June.

DEB. First phase?

NASREEN. Yes.

DEB *nods slowly, gazing at* NASREEN. NASREEN *smiles, unsure.* DEB *roots in her bag and takes out a bottle of water. She opens it and takes a swig.*

DEB. What school's he at? Your... What were it?

NASREEN. Sanjay.

DEB. Sanjay.

NASREEN. Leeds Grammar.

DEB. How'd you wangle that one then?

She takes another swig of water.

NASREEN. We pay. It's an independent school.

DEB. Private.

NASREEN. Yes.

DEB *nods then screws the cap on the water. She drops her bottle into her bag.*

DEB. 'Un he's up the Grammar School already, is he?

NASREEN. I'm sorry…? Oh, no it's not a secondary school. Well, it is, but Sanjay's a junior. The 'grammar' thing… It doesn't mean anything. It's just a name.

DEB nods, staring at NASREEN.

DEB. Is that right?

NASREEN. It… Yeah.

DIANNA *returns with* STEPHIE. *She puts the crib sheets on the table.*

DIANNA. Crib sheets.

She looks back and forth at NASREEN *and* DEB. DEB *looks away.*

Right. Let's make a start.

DIANNA *goes to the flip chart and picks up a pen.*

So, the idea of the game… Sorry to go over old ground, Nasreen.

NASREEN. Oh, no. Fine. Think I'm going to need all the help I can get.

She smiles at DEB. *The sentiment is not returned.*

DIANNA. Okay. The object of the game is to win as many tricks as possible in order to score points. Or, if you're defending, what you're aiming to do is stop your oppenents.

STEPHIE. Doin' what?

DIANNA. Taking tricks.

DEB. Scoring points.

DIANNA. It all amounts to the same thing in the end.

DEB. Does it?

DIANNA. Yes. So. What we're going to be looking at this evening is…

She taps the chart with her pen.

Dealing. And… (*Taps the board.*) The auction.

STEPHIE. Auction?

NASREEN. Or bidding. Some people call it bidding.

DIANNA. They do indeed.

   DIANNA *scrawls 'Bidding', across the board.*

STEPHIE. Right.

DIANNA. This is when we decide our trump suit and how
   many tricks we will make.

STEPHIE. Y... eah. Ought we be writing this down?

DEB. It's not rocket science, is it?

   DIANNA *gives* DEB *a fixed smile.*

DIANNA. It just requires a little application. So. In order to
   decide our trumps...

   STEPHIE *puts her hand up.*

DEB. Just ask.

   STEPHIE *puts her hand down.*

STEPHIE. Yeah. Sorry. No, but the thing is... Trumps, right?
   Can you remind us? It's ages since I played cards.

DIANNA. Of course. Nasreen, perhaps you'd like to explain?

   All eyes on NASREEN.

NASREEN. Oh. Yes. A trump is a card from the suit that's been
   chosen to rank above the others.

DEB. So, what, you give it more status than what it's really
   worth?

   NASREEN *fixes* DEB *with a steady gaze.*

NASREEN. Yes.

DIANNA. But, perhaps, the most important thing to remember
   is that it can take a trick where a card of a different suit has
   been led.

DEB. You score more points with it.

NASREEN. Take tricks.

DIANNA. Yes, as Nasreen perhaps more accurately suggests, you take tricks with it.

STEPHIE. Do what?

DIANNA. We're getting ahead of ourselves.

DEB. I'm not. I'm fine.

STEPHIE. I'm struggling.

DIANNA. Let's backtrack a bit.

DEB looks away.

Deb?

DEB. Not fussed.

An exaggerated yawn.

DIANNA. Essentially then, the game of contract bridge is divided into four distinct stages.

Flips page over to a clean sheet.

Stage one: dealing.

Scrawls on the chart.

Stage two?

NASREEN. The auction.

A look from DEB.

STEPHIE. Bidding.

DIANNA. Excellent. The auction – (*Taps chart.*) or, as Stephie says, the bidding. The next stage is…

NASREEN. Playing your hand.

STEPHIE. Feel I should be getting this down.

DEB. It's up there. (*On the board.*)

STEPHIE. Yeah, but… Yeah.

DIANNA. And last but most certainly not least…

DEB. Scoring.

STEPHIE (*nodding*). Scoring.

DIANNA. Now what we're going to be focusing on this evening is dealing and an introduction to the auction.

STEPHIE. Bidding.

> DEB *throws her a look.*

> That's its other name, int it?

DEB. Yeah, but you don't have to keep repeating everything.

STEPHIE. I'm tryin' to learn it.

DIANNA. Now if you'd like to take a look at the crib sheets I gave you.

> NASREEN *hands around the crib sheets.*

STEPHIE. Us two'll share.

DIANNA. There's no need.

STEPHIE. It's just…

> *She exchanges a look with* DEB.

> Her sight's not great in this light.

> DEB *snatches the crib sheet towards them.*

DIANNA. Looking at the top of sheet one, you'll see I've ranked the cards in order of status. Spades and hearts are your major suits and diamonds and clubs are the minors.

STEPHIE. So a heart's worth more than a diamond?

DIANNA. Yes.

DEB. 'Un a spade's stronger than a club.

DIANNA. Exactly. You'll soon get the hang of it.

STEPHIE's mobile phone goes. It's clear from DIANNA's reaction that mobiles are not de rigueur at the bridge club.

STEPHIE. I'll 'ave to get this. Sorry. Hiya, love.

She gets up from the table and walks around as she speaks.

You'll have to shout, I can't… (*Shouting.*) You what? Not now I can't, no. I'm playing bridge with… Eh? BRIDGE! It is, yeah. That's exactly it, like whist only worse. Yeah?

Rolls her eyes and mouths 'Sorry'.

How'd you go on? No! Aw, that's brilliant. (*Aside, pointing at the phone.*) It's me son. Jack. He's just… What? (*To JACK.*) Is he? Yeah, go on then put him on. Si? He has, yeah. Aw, I am, I'm chuffed to bits, yeah. I'm playing bridge. Yeah, you do, I told you before I come out. Yeah, we're not doing too bad. Deb. It's… Yeah, it's early days.

DIANNA looks at her watch and picks up the cards.

'Bout ten o'clock, yeah. We will do, crack open a bottle of that fizzy wine I got the other weekend. Celebrate. Bye, love. Bye, bye.

Hangs up and sits back in her chair with a big grin on her face.

DEB. What?

DIANNA taps the cards on the table.

STEPHIE. They're through!

DEB. Great.

STEPHIE. Our Jack's made it through to the finals.

DIANNA. I'm sorry…?

STEPHIE. Maths challenge…

DIANNA. Oh!

DIANNA puts the cards back on the table.

STEPHIE. And his team have made it through to the final round. National final.

DIANNA. Really? That's wonderful. Congratulations.

NASREEN. Which school is he at?

STEPHIE. Just the local comp up from ours but he's doing all right.

DIANNA. Evidently. It's not…? Jack Armstrong! Of course. You're Jack's mum. I teach him. Maths. I'm his maths teacher.

STEPHIE. No way. Are ya?

DIANNA. Yes.

STEPHIE. Hey, Deb.

DEB. I 'eard.

STEPHIE. What d'you think to that?

DEB *shrugs*.

DEB. What'm I s'posed to think?

STEPHIE. She's our Jack's teacher.

DEB. Yeah, you've just said.

DIANNA. It didn't occur to me when I saw the surname but I can see it now.

STEPHIE. They do say he's more my side. To look at anyhow.

DEB. What, so you never went to parents' evening then?

DIANNA. There isn't one. Not until the spring.

DEB. How come?

DIANNA. The autumn term's such a nightmare.

DEB *stares at her.*

Busy. I meant busy. But in any case, it's better for the students.

DEB. Is it?

DIANNA. Well, I think so. It gives them a little time to settle in before we meet the parents. It can be quite daunting for some of them, moving up to the middle school. But Jack's risen to the challenge brilliantly. I think he's probably one of the brightest students we've ever had.

STEPHIE. No. Go on. Really?

DIANNA. Absolutely.

STEPHIE *beams*.

STEPHIE. Dead proud of him.

NASREEN. You must be.

STEPHIE *catches* DEB*'s eye*.

STEPHIE. But whatever they're like, you still love 'em, don't you?

DEB *picks her nails*.

NASREEN. Of course.

DEB. Majors and minors?

STEPHIE. Can't believe it. (*Shaking her head*.) Our Jack of all people.

DEB. The cards?

DIANNA. Oh, yes. Let's crack on. Okay, I think p'raps…

Glances at her watch.

STEPHIE. What would me mam think to that I wonder…

DIANNA. The best way to learn is to play, so let's do a little dummy run. Practice run. As it were.

STEPHIE*'s still basking in her glory*.

DEB. Yeah, good idea.

DIANNA *picks up the cards and shuffles them with an expert flourish. She spreads the cards out across the table*.

DIANNA. What we need to do first is establish our partners. We'll each draw a card and the two with the highest cards will play the two with the lowest. Okay?

DEB. Think I've got that, yeah.

DIANNA. Good.

STEPHIE *snaps out of her reverie*.

STEPHIE. Can't we choose?

DIANNA. You can do.

DEB. Sooner you done it. Decided.

DIANNA. Let's see what the cards say.

STEPHIE. D'you ever 'ave 'em read? Your cards.

DEB. They're playing cards, not tarot cards.

STEPHIE. Talking though, aren't they? The cards.

DEB. No. It's us what's talking.

STEPHIE. Communicating.

DEB. Yes.

DIANNA. It's fascinating. A couple of sessions and you'll be hooked, trust me. Right. If you'd each like to take a card.

DEB *takes a card*. NASREEN *takes a card*. STEPHIE *takes two cards by mistake*.

STEPHIE. Oops. I've took two by mistake look. Tell you what, I'll just pop this one back in…

She shoves the card back into the pack and knocks half a dozen or so on the floor.

DEB. Stephanie.

DIANNA *bends down and picks up the stray cards*.

STEPHIE. I'm sorry, love.

DEB. D'you wanna reshuffle?

DIANNA. No, no. Let's press on.

DIANNA draws a card.

So. What have we got?

NASREEN. King of spades.

STEPHIE. Queen of hearts.

DIANNA. And I've got the six of diamonds. Deb?

DEB. Ten.

She turns the card around to show the girls.

Clubs.

STEPHIE. Which is a minor, int it?

DIANNA. Yes. However, since it's clear that the king and queen are higher than the ten and the six...

She cocks her head at DEB.

DEB. I'm with you. (*A forced smile.*) Thanks.

DIANNA. Then whether the cards are major or minor suits is immaterial. So, it looks to me as if Nasreen and Stephie are partners and Deb plays with me.

STEPHIE. Short straw. Sorry.

NASREEN smiles.

NASREEN. Not at all.

DIANNA looks at DEB.

DEB. Doesn't bother me, why would it?

DIANNA. Good. Right, ladies. Musical chairs.

She gets up.

DEB. Eh?

NASREEN gets up.

STEPHIE. What we doin' now?

NASREEN. We need to sit opposite one another.

STEPHIE. Do we? Why?

NASREEN. We're partners?

STEPHIE. Oh, yeah. I'm with you. [I understand.]

> STEPHIE *and* DEB *get up. General confusion for a moment or two.* STEPHIE *hoots with laughter.*

What're we like?

> *They settle into their seats, relieved to have established who should be sitting where with whom.*

DIANNA. Excellent. Nasreen? You're dealer.

DEB. How come?

DIANNA. She drew the highest card.

DEB. Right.

STEPHIE. Does it matter then? Who deals?

DIANNA. Not really. Everyone gets a turn.

DEB. And she's going first?

DIANNA. Yes.

DEB. Go on then.

DIANNA. One moment. If you'd like to cut, Deb?

DEB. How'd you mean? 'Cut.'

> DIANNA *demonstrates cutting the cards. She gestures for* DEB *to do it.*

No point. You've done it now.

STEPHIE. Don't be childish.

DEB. I'm not being childish, I'm…

> DIANNA *getures to* NASREEN *to deal.*

DIANNA. Nasreen?

NASREEN *deals the cards*. DEB *snatches hers up*.
STEPHIE *takes her cards*.

STEPHIE. Thanks, love.

DIANNA. If you'd like to arrange your cards in suits first. And
then arrange them on the table in front of you so that you've
got a red suit then a black suit, then another red and a black.
Like so.

She demonstrates.

It's just for ease of reference. We'll play with open hands for
the time being.

STEPHIE. How'd you mean, 'open'.

DEB. Face up so everyone can see what you've got.

STEPHIE (*making a bungled attempt to arrange her cards*).
Struggling here. Whoops.

Drops a card.

DIANNA. You'll soon get the hang of it. Get yourself a pack of
cards and practise at home.

STEPHIE *retrieves the card*.

STEPHIE. I will do. Use me son's.

Pops cards back in her hand.

He plays poker.

DEB. Mine does an' all.

STEPHIE. He's dead good at it.

DEB. Luck, int it?

DIANNA. To a certain extent.

DEB. Depends on your hand.

STEPHIE. Won a load of stuff.

NASREEN. They gamble?

STEPHIE. Bits and pieces. Music and the like. Games, that sort of thing. Not money. Wouldn't want him doing that.

DIANNA. It can't buy happiness.

DEB. Made a world of difference to me.

STEPHIE. D'you think?

    STEPHIE *gazes at* DEB *for a moment.*

DEB. I do, yeah. Changed me life.

    STEPHIE *nods slowly. She looks back at her cards.*

DIANNA. Okay, what you need to do next is to add up your points.

STEPHIE. We've not started playing yet.

NASREEN. Calculate what your hand's worth. The cards you're holding? You need to establish what they're worth.

STEPHIE. R… ight.

DIANNA. If you'd just like to refer to your sheets, you'll see that…

STEPHIE. Knows all this stuff, our Jack. (*Playful shrug.*) Not like his mother.

DEB. No.

STEPHIE. Anything to do with numbers 'un he's there, you know. His thing, numbers. Dead proud of him. Chuffed to bits.

    Studying her sheet.

DIANNA. Yes. So looking at the sheet, you'll see that an ace is worth…

STEPHIE. Deserves it, mind, because he's worked that hard.

DIANNA. Good. Right.

STEPHIE. Dedication, int it? Having a goal and sticking to it. Because to my mind…

DEB. Are we counting our points, or what?

DEB *lays her cards on the table*.

DIANNA. We are. Now, let's see what…

She puts her cards on the table.

DEB. Fifteen. And I've got a long suit. I get 'nother point for that, don't I?

STEPHIE *looks down at her cards*.

STEPHIE. Done what?

DIANNA. Let's keep it simple for the time being.

STEPHIE *counts her points*.

STEPHIE. Seven.

NASREEN. Nine.

STEPHIE. Your Paul done all right, though, hasn't he? Now that he's up that special school.

DEB. Sports academy.

STEPHIE. Lot better off up there. Because to my mind with someone like Paul, the normal system's just setting 'em up to fail, int it?

DEB *pushes her chair back from the table*.

DEB. Need a smoke. D'you mind?

STEPHIE. What, now? You'll interrupt the game.

DEB. I just need a bit of air.

DIANNA. It is a little oppressive in here.

DEB. 'Tis, yeah.

STEPHIE. D'you want a glass of water?

DEB. No.

DEB *gets up*. STEPHIE *makes as if to get up*.

STEPHIE. I'll come.

DEB. You're all right.

STEPHIE. Company.

DEB. I'm going for a smoke, for chrissakes.

STEPHIE *sits back down*.

DIANNA. We'll hang on till you get back.

NASREEN. Of course.

DEB *rummages for her fags and exits*. STEPHIE *gazes after her*.

STEPHIE. Think it's the move.

NASREEN. Isn't she happy then?

STEPHIE. Left a lot of stuff behind.

NASREEN. Memories?

STEPHIE. She'll be all right.

DIANNA. Is she on her own?

STEPHIE. Just her and Paul.

DIANNA. Her son?

STEPHIE. Yeah.

A pause.

He died, Rob did.

NASREEN. Her partner?

STEPHIE. Husband.

DIANNA. How old was he?

STEPHIE. Thirty-four.

DIANNA. How dreadful.

DEB *comes back in. The others freeze*. DEB *snatches her matches off the table*.

DEB. Matches.

She shakes the matches.

Forgot 'em.

STEPHIE. Right.

DEB. What?

STEPHIE. Nothing.

NASREEN. We were just chatting.

DIANNA. You go and enjoy your smoke.

DEB. Why?

NASREEN. We can wait.

DEB. No, you're all right. (*Re: her craving.*) It's gone off now.

STEPHIE. Go and have a fag.

DEB. No.

> DEB *sits down at the table.*

I'm stopping.

STEPHIE. We weren't talking about you.

DIANNA. Let's crack on.

DEB. You what? No, hold on a minute, will you? What's been said?

STEPHIE. Nothing's been said. About what?

> DEB *stares at* STEPHIE.

I were just… We were talking about the kids that's all.

DEB. Paul and Jack?

STEPHIE. Well, yeah.

DIANNA. Stephie just explained about your husband.

NASREEN. I'm sorry.

DIANNA. Yes. It must be difficult for you.

DEB. We manage.

NASREEN. I'm sure you do.

> DEB *throws* NASREEN *a look.*

STEPHIE. Thought they should know.

DEB. Why?

STEPHIE. In case you're off wi' 'em.

DEB. Am I?

   A pause.

DIANNA. We were a bit concerned.

DEB. About what? I went for a fag. Jesus.

   NASREEN *glances at her watch.*

   Yeah, good idea.

DIANNA. So, Deb. Starting with you. Fifteen points, you say?

DEB. I 'ave, yeah.

DIANNA. Okay.

STEPHIE. Sorry.

DEB. Forget it. I… Yeah, I am bit cranky. I'm sorry.

   STEPHIE *reaches for* DEB's *hand.* DEB *snatches it away, then gestures 'Don't'.*

DIANNA. Let's focus on our cards, shall we?

   DEB *nods.* STEPHIE *stares at her cards.*

STEPHIE. Don't know what to do.

DEB. Nothing. You don't have to *do* anything.

   STEPHIE *looks up at* DEB.

STEPHIE. Wanna help you.

DEB. I'm fine.

STEPHIE (*to* DIANNA *and* NASREEN). I'm sorry.

DEB. What you apologising for?

NASREEN. There's no need.

DIANNA. We've all been there.

DEB *looks at* DIANNA.

Lost someone.

DEB. Have you?

NASREEN. Not yet.

DEB. She… We both of us…

STEPHIE. Yeah. Long, long time ago now, though, eh?

DEB. I… Yeah. Sorry.

STEPHIE. No bother. Lost me mam as a kid. Fine about it.

She smiles.

You move on.

DEB *looks away.*

DIANNA. It's entirely understandable, your… [behaviour.]

DEB. What?

NASREEN. It must be hard for you, bringing him up alone.

DEB *stares at* NASREEN.

DIANNA. Let's press on, shall we? Fifteen points.

DEB. Fifteen.

DIANNA. Well. That's not a bad hand.

STEPHIE. 'Un I've got seven.

DIANNA. Nasreen?

NASREEN. Nine.

DIANNA. And I have nine too. Okay, let's start the bidding.

Scene Two

Several weeks later. Function room as before. On the flip chart, scrawled in DIANNA*'s ubiquitous green ink is: 'Beginners' Bridge. Week Six: Pre-emptive bidding'. The girls are standing in a group drinking tea out of disposable cups.*

STEPHIE. Still don't get why I'd wanna be bidding at level three.

DIANNA. It's a pre-emptive bid.

STEPHIE. Yeah, but why though?

NASREEN. To shut out the opposition when you're weak.

STEPHIE. Okay.

DIANNA. Do you see?

Beat.

STEPHIE. No.

DIANNA. By opening with a bid of three or more, you're preventing your opponents bidding.

STEPHIE. But I only had nine points.

DIANNA. So you're weak. But, you had a long, strong suit.

STEPHIE. Seven spades.

NASREEN. With the ace and the king.

DIANNA. Which means if spades are trumps you're still in with a good chance.

DEB. Yeah? [Do you understand?]

Pause.

STEPHIE. No.

DEB. Aw, Stephanie!

STEPHIE. Sorry.

DIANNA. We all learn at different rates.

STEPHIE. S'pose. Speaking of which. (*To* NASREEN.) Have you told her?

NASREEN. Excuse me?

DEB. What?

STEPHIE. Oh, you must tell her.

NASREEN. I don't know what you're talking about.

STEPHIE. Yeah, you do. *Look North* last night. (*To* DIANNA.) Did you not see it?

DIANNA. Not last night, no.

STEPHIE. She's only been on telly. This one.

DEB. She has? How come?

NASREEN. Some coverage about the NAGC. We were interviewed.

DIANNA. Really? How exciting. Your son's a member, is he?

NASREEN. Yes.

DEB. The what?

DIANNA. The National Association for Gifted Children.

DEB *nods*.

NASREEN. It's nothing really.

STEPHIE. Yeah, it is. Course it is. You were on the telly!

DEB. Never seen it.

STEPHIE. No, but listen to this, right? Listen. Her... Sunil.

NASREEN. Sanjay. Sunil's my husband.

STEPHIE. Course he is. Sorry, love, getting 'em mixed up. I'm rubbish with names, me. Her Sanjay done his maths GCSE already. Seven-year-old.

DIANNA. Terrific! You must be thrilled.

NASREEN. We're… Yes, we're very proud.

STEPHIE. What grade did he get?

NASREEN. Oh, he hasn't taken it yet. Next June.

STEPHIE. Even so. Hey, p'raps he can teach two of us to play bridge.

NASREEN. Chess is more his game.

STEPHIE. And he's only seven-year-old. Imagine. Might get our Jack to practise with me at home.

DIANNA. Does he play?

STEPHIE. Dabbles a bit online. He'd pick it up dead quick if he was here.

DIANNA. Perhaps you should introduce Sanjay to the game, Nasreen, then the four of you could get together.

NASREEN. I might just do that.

STEPHIE. What… With me, you mean?

NASREEN. Why ever not?

DEB *throws* STEPHIE *a look*.

STEPHIE. Just… Yeah. No reason.

DEB. What, round at hers, would you?

NASREEN. If Stephie wouldn't mind?

STEPHIE. Course. You'd be very welcome…

DEB. Yeah, right.

STEPHIE. …love.

NASREEN. Thanks.

DEB. You don't want her coming round yours then?

NASREEN. Not at the moment. No.

STEPHIE. Mum's not well. Nasreen's.

DEB. Yeah, you said. (*Beat.*) I'm sorry.

NASREEN *nods*.

STEPHIE. Be fine. Playing round ours.

DEB (*aside to* STEPHIE). What you on? [What are you thinking?]

DIANNA. It'd be great practice for you both.

> DEB *gets out her ciggies.* DIANNA *picks up a Tupperware box and hands it to* DEB.

> Cookie?

> DEB *peers at the biscuits*.

DEB. You're all right, thanks.

DIANNA. Watching your waistline?

DEB. No.

> DIANNA *offers the box to* STEPHIE *and* NASREEN, *who each take one*.

STEPHIE. D'you bake 'em yourself?

DIANNA. Huh, I wish.

STEPHIE. They look… Real.

DIANNA. Little farm shop down the road.

NASREEN. Roundstones?

> NASREEN *takes a bite*.

DIANNA. Yes.

NASREEN (*catching crumbs as she speaks through a mouthful*). I know the one.

DEB. You shop there?

NASREEN. We supply them.

DEB. What with?

NASREEN. My husband's a '*Purveyor of fine Indian wines*'. They're one of his best customers.

DEB. Is that what he does then?

NASREEN (*brushing crumbs off her clothes*). It's his business, yes.

DEB. Didn't know you drank wine.

NASREEN. I don't.

DEB. But he does?

NASREEN. Sunil's a Hindu.

DEB. What are you?

DIANNA. Nasreen's a Muslim.

Beat.

NASREEN. Yes.

DEB. How does that work?

NASREEN. We love each other.

DEB *nods*.

DEB. You must row though.

NASREEN. Doesn't everyone?

DEB. S'pose.

STEPHIE. God, we do. Bloody hell. You did an' all.

DEB. We… Yeah, we did.

A pause.

STEPHIE. Still misses him.

DEB. Well, yeah…?

NASREEN *nods*.

You get on with it. You have to.

NASREEN. Did you get any professional help?

DEB. He's dead.

A pause.

NASREEN. There are people who can help.

DEB. Professional people? What, like doctors, you mean?

STEPHIE *takes a bite of her biscuit.*

STEPHIE. These are nice. Walnuts is it?

DIANNA. Brazils.

STEPHIE. What other stuff do they do?

DIANNA. Fruit and veg, cheese and the bread's to die for.

STEPHIE. Get all mine on staff discount at work.

DIANNA. That makes sense.

STEPHIE. Yeah, but it's nice to 'ave a change, though, int it?
Something a bit special.

STEPHIE *dunks the biscuit into her cup.* DEB *throws her a look.*

What? Oh, sorry I always...

STEPHIE *peers into her cup.*

Sorry.

DIANNA. They're very crumbly. Let me get you a fresh one.
[Cup of tea.]

STEPHIE. No, you're all right, thanks.

STEPHIE *puts her cup back on the table.* DEB *snatches it up
and goes across to a bin to throw the cup away.* STEPHIE
rubs the baize top as if in an effort to remove a stain. DEB
comes back.

You wanna get some them biscuits, Deb. Chutneys. Jams.
Love all that stuff, me.

NASREEN. Traditional '*fayre*'.

STEPHIE. Bet they've got a nice little café an' all. Have they?

DIANNA. It's a bit pricey.

DEB. Get what you pay for.

DIANNA. Yes.

STEPHIE. Might give it a go on the weekend. It's gonna chuck it down next couple of weeks, so Si'll be picking up a load of fares and I've got me bit of overtime. (*To* DEB.) Covering for Selma. 'Nother one on the way.

Playful shrug.

DEB. Yeah, well.

STEPHIE. Suits us. Need the money.

DIANNA. What does your husband do?

DEB. Taxi driver.

DIANNA. Interesting.

DEB. Is it?

STEPHIE. He enjoys it.

DIANNA. Good.

DEB. Political an' all, her husband. He...

STEPHIE. Watches all them programmes. *Question Time*. Then that other one. 'From Downing Street, to your street.'

NASREEN. *The Politics Show.*

STEPHIE. Think it's Simon what give Jack his brains. He's dead good with numbers an' all. Money and stuff. And his memory, he knows this city like the back of his hand. Name you any street you like. So, yeah, it's him he takes after. Not his mother, that's for sure.

DIANNA. Well. You should be very proud of him. I'm sure he's bound for great things.

STEPHIE. I'm... Yeah, he's a good lad. He's always liked sums. Right from tiny.

DIANNA. We've got a really strong team this year. I think we've got every chance.

STEPHIE. You going an' all then?

DIANNA. Myself and another member of staff.

DEB. Nice little jolly for you.

DEB reaches for a biscuit.

DIANNA. What about Paul?

DEB. Maths? Jokin' me.

Breaks the biscuit in two.

DIANNA. What are his interests? Any after-school activities?

STEPHIE. Loves his sport.

DEB. Yeah. That and the telly.

DEB brushes the crumbs from her jeans.

He likes the animal programmes.

STEPHIE. And *X Factor.*

DEB. Your Jack likes that.

DIANNA. I think they all do.

DEB. Do they?

DEB puts a piece of biscuit in her mouth.

Wouldn't know.

STEPHIE. All Jack's mates watch it.

DIANNA. I don't know many that don't.

STEPHIE. Aw, but he's dead good at sport though. Your Paul.

DEB takes a minute to respond. Her mouth's full of something that tastes a bit like sawdust.

DEB. Yeah, he's… Yeah, he's not bad.

She picks her teeth.

STEPHIE. Not bad! Tell 'em, will you?

DEB. Been spotted by some scout.

STEPHIE. Talent scout. For cricket. He's gonna play for county.

DIANNA. Oh, my goodness!

DEB. Might do, yeah.

NASREEN. Really?

DEB *throws her a look.*

How wonderful.

DIANNA. You must be thrilled.

DEB. I'm... Yeah, I am, I'm pretty proud of him really.

NASREEN. So cricket's his sport, is it?

DEB. That 'un football.

STEPHIE. Oh, he's dead good at football.

DEB. He is, yeah. Might make professional one day.

NASREEN. He'll earn a fortune and look after you.

DEB. Don't need looking after.

STEPHIE. Financially secure.

DEB *throws her a look.*

Well, yeah, because of...

DEB. Me husband's life insurance.

STEPHIE. Sorry.

DEB. Five hundred thousand. Bit like winning the lottery.

STEPHIE. You've had to fight 'em for ev'ry penny of that money.

DEB *throws her a look.*

But they paid up in the end and that's the main thing.

DIANNA. Sounds as if you've been through a lot.

DEB *shrugs.*

NASREEN. Yes. It must've been terrible for you, Deb.

STEPHIE. But she's put it all behind her now.

Beat.

DEB. I 'ave done, yeah.

A pause.

NASREEN. My husband plays cricket at the local club. You should get Paul to come along. They're very friendly.

STEPHIE *throws* DEB *a look.*

DEB. You're all right, thanks.

NASREEN *nods.*

NASREEN. Right. Well, if you change your mind…

STEPHIE. Oh no, it's not that she's racist or nothing, it's just… Well, it's a bit awkward, love, int it?

DEB. Tell 'em every bloody thing, why don't you?

DIANNA *drains her cup and glances at her watch.*

STEPHIE. Weren't his fault though, were it? You know what they're like, these young lads.

DEB. He got an ASBO. Last summer.

STEPHIE. Over some girl.

Knowing looks from DIANNA *and* NASREEN.

DEB. No. Well, yeah but… Yeah.

STEPHIE. He's not a bad lad, Paul.

DEB. No.

STEPHIE. Wouldn't never 'ave happened had the brother not…

DEB. My Paul weren't to blame.

STEPHIE. Course not, no. (*Beat.*) Well, you can't be with 'em ev'ry minute of the day. Not at fourteen.

DEB. I know me own son, all right? But… yeah, he is, he's to be in by nine on this ASBO. So, thanks for the offer but no thanks.

NASREEN. I understand.

DEB *throws her a 'Like hell you do' look.*

DIANNA. Half-past, ladies. Think p'raps we should...

DEB. I'm not finished me tea yet.

DIANNA. Oh, I'm sorry. No rush.

DIANNA *begins to scrutinise the noticeboard.*

STEPHIE. Load of stuff goin' on.

DIANNA. Yes. Plenty to do. I don't understand why anyone would want to get involved with this lot though.

DEB. What, the rally you mean?

STEPHIE. Eh?

DEB. BNP rally.

STEPHIE. Oh, that. God, no. I wouldn't wanna go to that. Wants stoppin' if you ask me.

NASREEN. I think it's important. Freedom of expression.

DEB. *You* do?

STEPHIE. You're not... Yeah, but you're not a member.

NASREEN. No, but we live in a democracy.

DIANNA. Well, I... Yes, I agree but... The BNP, for heavenssakes.

NASREEN. Obviously I don't agree with what they stand for but I don't want to live in a police state. So long as it's a peaceful demonstration.

STEPHIE. Oh, it will be. From what I gather, like. Stuff in press. Local radio.

DEB. Not into it meself. Politics. They none of 'em mean what they say so what's point?

DIANNA. We can't afford to be complacent.

DEB. You what?

NASREEN. I don't think Dianna meant...

DEB. I think I know what she meant, thanks.

DIANNA. It's terrifying, the support they're getting.

STEPHIE. They wouldn't get my vote. Bane of me life.

DIANNA. Really?

DEB. Simon. Her husband.

DIANNA. He's going along, is he?

STEPHIE. He… Yeah, he might.

DEB. Stephie.

STEPHIE. Yes.

DIANNA. I see.

DEB. Do you?

STEPHIE. I don't agree with his views and if I could I'd change them but…

DIANNA. I'm sorry, I couldn't live with that.

DEB. You don't have to.

DIANNA. Nor does Stephie.

STEPHIE. He's my husband.

DIANNA. Come on, Stephie, it's the twenty-first century.

DEB. When did love go out of fashion?

DIANNA. I'm sorry…?

DEB. I said when did love go out of fashion?

DIANNA. I just don't see how you can have a relationship with someone whose views you're completely opposed to.

DEB (*re* NASREEN). She does.

STEPHIE. Deborah.

DEB. I'm sticking up for you.

STEPHIE. Don't need stickin' up for.

DEB. You in one? A relationship.

DIANNA. l look after my disabled mother.

DEB *studies her cup for a moment then screws it up and dumps it in the bin.*

STEPHIE. Lovely. Looking after your mum. How old is she?

DIANNA. Ninety-two.

STEPHIE. Ninety-two.

A long pause.

I don't vote for 'em

DEB. You don't vote.

STEPHIE. No. But if I did, I wouldn't. Because I don't agree with their views.

DIANNA. What about Jack?

DEB. What about him?

DIANNA. I'm asking Stephie.

DEB. What are you asking her?

STEPHIE. I can speak!

DEB. Go on then.

STEPHIE. What?

DIANNA. I was wondering what effect it might have on Jack?

NASREEN. Your husband's involvement with the BNP.

STEPHIE. None so's you'd notice.

DIANNA. You don't discuss it?

STEPHIE. No. He's got a load of coloured friends though.

DIANNA *looks away.*

NASREEN. I find it very difficult sometimes. With Sunil's business. I do understand.

DIANNA *looks back.*

DIANNA. Oh, come on.

NASREEN. Excuse me...?

DIANNA. I just don't buy that, I'm afraid. Her husband's in the BNP!

NASREEN. She's not. You can't blame Stephie for what her husband believes in.

DIANNA. She's condoning it. As good as.

NASREEN. No, she isn't. I don't agree with Sunil's views on alcohol at all. We row about it constantly but that doesn't change the way I feel about him. (*To* STEPHIE.) It's very difficult for you, I can see that.

STEPHIE. It... Yeah. It's a bit tricky sometimes. Thanks, love.

NASREEN *smiles at* STEPHIE.

NASREEN. People are quick to judge. The number of times it's compromised me professionally...

DEB. Because your husband sells booze?

NASREEN. Yes.

DEB. Up to him, int it?

NASREEN. No. It's up to us.

DEB. You turn a blind eye.

NASREEN. Yes.

Pause.

DIANNA. It's not the same thing at all.

NASREEN. The issues are very different but...

DIANNA. I'm sorry.

She throws STEPHIE *a look.*

I just...

STEPHIE*'s phone goes. She fumbles in her bag and snatches it out.*

STEPHIE. Hiya, love. You what? You're very crackly. You driving? Not with a fare. Pull over. If you get stopped. Ah, no, c'mon, will you, we can't afford for you to… Eh? When? Is he all right? Thank God.

NASREEN. Stephie?

STEPHIE. This lad's been attacked up the school.

NASREEN. Not Jack?

STEPHIE. Si? Can you hear me? Oh. Good. What now? Yeah, course, I'll get me… [stuff.] So, is he… A what?

STEPHIE *turns her back to the others.*

Right. Don't… No, don't muck about. He…

NASREEN *comes towards* STEPHIE.

You're breaking up. I can't hear you. Hello? Hello?

She drops the phone back in her bag.

Dead. Me phone.

DEB. Chrissakes, thought you meant… God, I dunno. Jesus, look at me hands. (*They're shaking*.)

NASREEN. Is everything all right?

STEPHIE. Fine. Well, no, not… Kid's been… I mean you don't, do you?

DEB. What?

STEPHIE. I don't know.

NASREEN. Let me get you a glass of water.

STEPHIE. No. Thank you.

NASREEN. I'll run you home.

STEPHIE. NO! Look, will you just… Just leave it, all right? I'm fine.

She starts to put her coat on.

DEB. I may's well come an' all.

STEPHIE. I don't want to spoil your evening.

DEB. You 'ave done. I'm comin'. On his way, is he?

STEPHIE *nods*.

STEPHIE. Just droppin' off a fare.

DEB. We'll wait out front.

STEPHIE *nods. They head for the door.*

DIANNA. He's not hurt?

STEPHIE. He'll be fine.

DIANNA. Well, that's a relief. You had us…

NASREEN. See you next week then?

DIANNA.…worried there for a minute. I do hope the other boy's all right.

STEPHIE. I… Yeah.

DEB. Where's his drop-off?

STEPHIE. Hangleton Road.

DEB. Five minutes then. Tops.

NASREEN. So, it's not Jack? Stephie? It's not Jack?

DEB *throws her a look.*

DIANNA. Deb?

DEB. Like I'm gonna bloody know. Taking her home.

DIANNA. I hope…

DEB. What?

DIANNA. I hope everything's okay.

DEB. Yeah, me an' all. C'mon, you.

DEB *and* STEPHIE *exit.* DIANNA *takes out her phone.*

DIANNA. Excuse me one moment.

NASREEN. Of course.

DIANNA (*on the phone*). Siobhan? Just this minute, yes. What happened? Who? How bad is it? Is he going to be all right? Right. Yes, I have. Nice family. His father's a… What, tomorrow morning? Yes. Yes, of course. Seven thirty in the staffroom. Sure, I'll be there. Yep, bye.

She hangs up.

New boy, year seven. Mohammed Sasooli.

NASREEN. I don't… Right. I don't know the name. Is he badly hurt?

DIANNA. She wouldn't say. Not over the phone. I'm going in first thing.

NASREEN. Right. Good.

Sound of a cab pulling up outside. They both gaze towards the door.

You don't think…

DIANNA. I don't know what to think.

NASREEN. No. Me neither.

The cab pulls away, its headlights flashing across the ceiling as it does so.

Scene Three

A couple of hours later. NASREEN *is clearing the tables and stacking chairs. The main lights have been switched off.* STEPHIE *appears in the doorway, silhouetted against the light from the corridor.*

STEPHIE. You're still here.

NASREEN. We were talking.

STEPHIE. You... Yeah, well, you would do.

> STEPHIE *enters.* NASREEN *picks up a chair and places it on the table.*

> I'm locked out. Si dropped us back from the hospital 'un I can't find me key. Thought p'raps I'd dropped it in 'ere.

NASREEN. I haven't seen it.

STEPHIE. Right.

> NASREEN *reaches for another chair.* STEPHIE *reaches out to help her.*

> D'you want a hand?

NASREEN. No.

> STEPHIE *withdraws her hand.* NASREEN *swings the chair onto the table with a thump.*

> Ask the caretaker. He's still here.

STEPHIE. Yeah, I... I'll... What, downstairs, is he?

> NASREEN *throws her a look.*

> Course.

NASREEN *picks up another chair.* STEPHIE *catches her eye.*

NASREEN. Tell me.

She lets the chair drop back to the floor.

I want to know what happened.

STEPHIE. They're keepin' him in overnight. It's just a precaution.

NASREEN. Mohammed?

Beat.

STEPHIE. Jack. Banged his head on a wall. This cut above his eye.

NASREEN. What happened to Mohammed? Mohammed Sasooli?

STEPHIE *drops her gaze.*

STEPHIE. I don't know. Don't know the lad. Do you?

NASREEN. No.

STEPHIE. Thought p'raps… Well, no, but his father's a doctor, you see.

NASREEN. Jack's implicated, isn't he?

STEPHIE. Police are gonna… They're gonna talk to him.

NASREEN. Question him?

STEPHIE. Yes. They're talking to everyone. Everyone that was there. There was… There was a gang of 'em.

NASREEN. You knew, didn't you? The minute you got that call, you knew.

STEPHIE. I don't *know* anything. No one does. Not yet.

NASREEN. You knew the boy was Asian.

STEPHIE. I did, yeah. I were in shock. Me son...

NASREEN. What?

STEPHIE. I weren't thinking straight, all right? I'm sorry, I would've said but... I were frightened.

NASREEN. Of what?

STEPHIE. Losing you.

NASREEN *nods.*

Have I?

NASREEN. Yes.

STEPHIE. Can't blame you.

NASREEN. Blame? Don't talk to me about blame. Oh, d'you know what? I'm not having this conversation.

STEPHIE. I'd feel same.

NASREEN. You don't know how I feel.

NASREEN *swings the chair up onto the table.*

STEPHIE. No.

NASREEN *moves towards* STEPHIE *to stack the chairs on the next table. She can't reach a chair in the corner next to* STEPHIE. *A moment's hesitation then* STEPHIE *passes her the chair.*

NASREEN. Thank you.

STEPHIE. Welcome.

NASREEN *puts the chair on the table and brushes her hands together as if to remove dust.*

He's... He's out of danger. The... You know. The little lad.

NASREEN. Mohammed.

STEPHIE. Yes.

NASREEN. He could've died then?

STEPHIE. He didn't. He won't. He's gonna be fine.

NASREEN. Is he? And what about Jack? What's going to happen to him?

STEPHIE. I don't know. He's just a kid.

NASREEN. He's fourteen.

STEPHIE. He's my son.

A pause.

I don't believe he done it. I just… He's never before in his life… I swear to God, Nasreen. I'm his mother.

NASREEN. Yes, you are.

STEPHIE. I know me own child.

NASREEN. I don't think you do. He could've died, Stephanie. Eleven years old and he could've died. What about his mother? What about her?

STEPHIE. But it… It don't make any sense. His best mate's a… He's Asian. He'd been… This afternoon, after school… They were… Whole gang of 'em, they were mucking about on the rec 'un then, 'cording to our Jack… These other ones come up the field and… He hit his head, he can't remember exactly what happened…

NASREEN. That's what he's said?

STEPHIE. Yeah and I believe him.

NASREEN. Do you?

STEPHIE. I don't honestly think it were him. He wouldn't. I mean, why would he?

NASREEN. You're asking me?

STEPHIE. No, but… God help me. I… I'm beside meself. I… I just… Please?

NASREEN. What?

STEPHIE. I don't know.

STEPHIE *breaks down.*

I'm sorry, Nasreen. I'm… I'm so sorry.

A long pause and then NASREEN *takes a chair off the table.*

NASREEN. D'you want to sit down?

STEPHIE *wipes her nose with her hand and nods.*
NASREEN *takes another chair off the table. They sit down.*
STEPHIE *wipes her nose with her hand again, then her eyes, her mouth…* NASREEN *passes her a tissue.* STEPHIE *nods. She can't speak.* NASREEN *gives her a moment to compose herself.*

There are professional services I can put you in touch with.

STEPHIE *looks at her.*

STEPHIE. No.

NASREEN. You need help.

STEPHIE. We'll manage.

NASREEN. You're not managing, are you? I… I just think you might benefit from some support.

STEPHIE. Thank you…

NASREEN. Good.

STEPHIE.…but I can't.

NASREEN. Why not?

Not once during the following exchange about her husband does STEPHIE *make eye contact with* NASREEN.

STEPHIE. It's… It's me husband. Simon.

NASREEN. Are you afraid of him?

STEPHIE. No.

NASREEN. Stephie? Has he ever…

STEPHIE. No, he wouldn't. He'd never do owt like that.

NASREEN. Does he threaten you?

STEPHIE *shakes her head.*

STEPHIE. Never.

NASREEN. I don't understand.

STEPHIE. Can't… [tell you.]

NASREEN. Yes you can. You can tell me, Stephie.

A long pause.

STEPHIE. They're me life, them two. Simon and… My Jack. There's nothing else.

STEPHIE *looks up at* NASREEN. *She holds her gaze for a moment or two before* NASREEN *looks away.*

Known him half me life. Grew up together.

NASREEN. Where did you meet?

STEPHIE. Primary school. Mixed infants. Girls and boys.

NASREEN. Of course.

STEPHIE. He made me laugh. Took me out meself. Helped me. Me… Me mam 'un that, you know.

NASREEN *nods.*

NASREEN. How old were you when she died?

STEPHIE. Eleven. Done all right though. Me grandma what brung us up. Till I was sixteen. But Si… Feels like he's always been there. Like if I… [left him.] Dunno what it'd all mean.

NASREEN. What?

STEPHIE. My life.

NASREEN. I think you need some help. Professional advice.

STEPHIE. No. Please?

She grabs NASREEN's *hand.*

They'll make me. They will, won't they?

NASREEN. They won't make you do anything you don't want to.

STEPHIE. I don't want them talking. Putting stuff in me head. Making me think things could be better. That I... I can't. I won't. I will not leave my husband. No. I'm sorry. I'm really, really sorry but...

NASREEN. What?

STEPHIE. I can't.

NASREEN. Why not?

STEPHIE. I love him.

A long pause.

NASREEN. If you love him. If you really love him? Then you must leave him.

STEPHIE. I don't want to be on me own.

STEPHIE *looks up at* NASREEN. NASREEN *holds her gaze.*

NASREEN. You won't be.

Scene Four

Several weeks later. Function room as before. On the chart, scrawled in green ink is: 'Beginners' Bridge. Week Twelve: Slam Methods'. Sound of a BNP rally taking place outside. It's clear from the noise that this is not a peaceful demonstration. DIANNA and DEB are sitting at the table. DEB is gazing towards the window.

DIANNA. Let's look at slams while we wait.

DEB. Eh?

DIANNA. Slams.

DEB. Oh, yeah.

DIANNA. So, what do we need for a slam?

DEB. Strong partnership. Thirty-three-plus points or... I'm sorry, just bit... [distracted.]

She crosses to the window and peers out.

Fuck! Sorry. They're chucking stuff and there's this one bloke...

DEB cranes to get a better view. DIANNA joins her at the window.

See him? That one there. He's bleeding.

DIANNA. Good God Almighty. Animals.

DEB glances at her watch.

She did say she might be a bit late.

DEB. Not to me she didn't. How come?

DIANNA. She needs to talk to Jack.

DEB. Why, what's he done now?

DIANNA. Nothing as far as I'm aware.

DEB. Seein' someone though, int he? Some woman.

DIANNA. So I believe.

DEB. Waste of space if you ask me. Counsellors. What do they bloody know?

DIANNA. Some people find it helpful.

DEB. I never. Anyhow, what I don't get, right?

DIANNA. Go on.

DEB. How come he's the one what's getting the help?

DIANNA. It's family therapy I believe.

DEB. What good's that gonna do?

DIANNA. Help them to communicate?

DEB. Fuck that. Sorry, but they wanna sort themselves out to my mind. I had to.

Beat.

DIANNA. Jack's been involved in a very serious crime...

DEB. We don't know that.

DIANNA. ...and, until the case goes to trial...

DEB. Not for sure.

DIANNA. ...they're wise to take all the help they can get.

DEB. I wouldn't want that. No way would I. Someone sticking their nose in.

DIANNA. Sometimes family is all you need.

DEB. Yeah, well.

DIANNA. I'm sorry, I didn't think.

DEB. Paul's mine. Family.

DIANNA. Yes. If ever you want to talk…?

DEB *nods*.

I can only imagine how difficult it must be.

DEB. It's… Yeah, it's not been easy.

DIANNA. How long have you been on your own?

DEB. I'm not on me own.

DIANNA. No.

DEB. Five years. Seems longer sometimes 'un then…

DIANNA. Like only yesterday?

DEB *nods*.

I know.

DEB. Yeah?

DIANNA. Yes.

A pause.

DEB. Right. I never…

DIANNA. That's okay. It was a long time ago. My fiancé was killed in the Falklands.

DEB. Squaddie?

DIANNA. He was in the army, yes.

DEB. You never forget.

DIANNA. No.

A long pause.

DEB. It were Paul's birthday. I'd an act booked. This clown. He were trying to get back for the party.

DIANNA. Robert?

DEB. Rob, yeah. It were a wet night. November. Freezing fog and this other truck coming in the opposite direction. Three-ton truck and he hit it head on.

DIANNA. How awful. I'm so sorry, Deb.

DEB. Weren't the crash what killed him. Not as such. He were thrown from cab. Silly beggar, weren't wearing his seat belt. If I'd told him once… Hyperthermia. They'd a devil of a job finding him and by the time they did… They explained it me up the hospital. This doctor.

DIANNA. It must be so difficult for them. Telling people.

DEB. Weren't no one's fault, he said. No one's to blame. The bastard.

DIANNA. You blame him?

DEB. His attitude. Cold. Distant. Like… Like as if Rob were just another job to him.

DIANNA. How else can you get through it? A job like that.

DEB. I don't know. I'm not a doctor. Not my problem, is it?

DIANNA. You mustn't blame him, Deb.

DEB. No. But I do.

DIANNA. He was only doing his job.

DEB. He was, yeah. Doin' what he's paid for.

DIANNA. Caring?

DEB. Yeah, right. Weren't a mark on him. I mean, you couldn't believe… They'd all this equipment and I says to him, I says can you not just give him one last chance. No, we've done everything we can. But he's in there, I says. I just… I just know it. He can't be dead. He can't be. Goes off home for his tea. 'Un my world, my life… It's nothing to him, is it? Nothing.

A long pause.

You know when you're vulnerable, right?

She wipes her nose on the back of her hand. DIANNA *takes a tissue from her bag and passes it to* DEB.

Ta. What does it mean again? Being vulnerable.

DIANNA. In bridge?

DEB. Well, yeah.

DIANNA *smiles*.

DIANNA. I shouldn't worry too much about vulnerability at this stage.

DEB. Thought we were doing all right.

DIANNA. Oh, absolutely. You've come on tremendously but anything to do with scoring I think we should leave for the time being. Just focus on bidding and how to play your hand. But, I have to say, you're beginning to communicate really effectively now. Most of the time your bidding is spot on.

DEB *wipes her eyes*.

DEB. I'm… Yeah, I'm getting the hang of it now.

Blows her nose. Chucks the tissue in bin.

Thought she would've been here by now.

DIANNA. Is she driving?

DEB. Bus. She doesn't drive. We neither of us took a test. Not that that stopped us when we were kids. Nothing did. Not then.

DEB *goes to the window and looks out*.

DIANNA. The bus stop isn't far.

DEB. Wouldn't wanna be out there now.

DIANNA. How did you get through?

DEB. I come in the back way. There's an alley from ours up to the tennis courts just round the back 'ere.

DIANNA. Is there?

DEB. Didn't you know that?

DIANNA. No.

DEB. Doubt she does either.

DEB *gets out her phone.* STEPHIE *bursts in.*

STEPHIE. Is she here yet? I seen her on…

Stripping off her things as she speaks.

…me way up.

DEB. Jesus, Stephie where the 'eck've you been?

STEPHIE. Have you seen what it's like out there?

DEB. That's what I bloody mean. Were dead worried about you.

STEPHIE. Yeah, thanks. Fine. Well, I'm 'ere, aren't I?

DEB. S'pose.

STEPHIE. So, yeah, I seen her on me way up. Stopped off for a packet of tea at the One Stop.

Dives to the window and looks up and down the street.

DEB. Did she?

STEPHIE. Me. I come out the shop and she'd gone. Just this heaving mass of bodies. Pushing, shoving, spitting. I couldn't move, breathe, nothing.

DEB. What's that on your coat?

STEPHIE. Egg.

STEPHIE *rubs at her coat. Chucks it down.*

It'll wash.

DIANNA. Oh, for heavenssakes.

STEPHIE. Yeah, they're chucking stuff.

She gets her phone out of her pocket and starts going through her contacts. DEB *throws her a look.*

DEB. Got her number then, 'ave you?

STEPHIE. Course.

DEB. Right.

STEPHIE. I'll phone her. She'll have her mobile. It's ringing. She'll of gone in a shop, won't she? There's that many of 'em out on street you can't put one foot in front the other. Oh! Voicemail.

She hangs up and drops the phone back in her pocket.

DEB. She'll be all right. What's the matter with you?

STEPHIE. Have you not seen 'em? Heard 'em. Listen. They're animals.

DEB. They've got it policed though. Dogs, horses… She'll be fine.

DIANNA. Try not to worry, Stephie. I'm sure she's perfectly capable of looking after herself.

STEPHIE. It's gone half-past. Twenty-five to when I seen her. That's an hour nearly.

DIANNA. Perhaps it was someone else you saw. It's difficult to tell in a crowd. Shall I phone her husband?

STEPHIE. No. He'll worry.

DEB. Not if she's sat at home.

STEPHIE. It was her. Definitely. She waved at us. Shouted across.

DEB. What did she say?

STEPHIE. I couldn't hear above the noise.

STEPHIE *snatches up her coat and heads for the door.*

DEB. What you doin'?

STEPHIE. I'm going to find her.

DIANNA. Don't be silly, Stephie. You'll never find her in that crowd.

STEPHIE. I can't stop in 'ere.

DEB. We are.

DEB *looks at* DIANNA.

DIANNA. Yes. We'd just be a nuisance out there on the street.

STEPHIE. I have to find her.

DEB. No you don't. Why?

STEPHIE. She's me friend.

> STEPHIE *exits.* DEB *stares after her.* DIANNA *gathers the cards.*

DIANNA. She won't find her.

DEB. She might.

> DIANNA *taps the cards on the table.*

DIANNA. She'll just be in the way.

> *She starts to shuffle the cards.*

Another body for the police to manage. It's the last thing they need.

DEB. It… Yeah. Think she wants to help.

DIANNA. Well… It won't. Slam. What's the first thing we need to agree on?

DEB. Trump suit or no trumps.

DIANNA. And secondly?

DEB. If we've got enough strength to go for it.

DIANNA. Excellent. Small slam?

DEB. Thirty-three points.

DIANNA. Grand slam?

DEB. Thirty-seven. Her Jack, right?

DIANNA. What?

DEB. Bit distracted. Sorry. No, but her Jack, yeah? I don't reckon he could of, do you? Done it I mean.

> *Unnoticed,* NASREEN *appears in the doorway.*

DIANNA. I've really no idea.

DEB. You must of talked about it though. Up the school.

DIANNA. We've had staff meetings.

DEB. Yeah, 'un you're only human. Like rest of us.

> DIANNA *looks at* DEB. *She holds her gaze for a moment then* DEB *looks away.*

> Must have a gut feeling. I 'ave.

DIANNA. It's evidence that counts in a case like this.

DEB. I've known him all his life. And all right so Simon's got his views an' that and Jack's no angel but beat an eleven-year-old kid half to death? He wouldn't do nothing like that. Not Jack.

DIANNA. There was CCTV footage. He was seen.

DEB. Well, yeah, he might've been there but…

DIANNA. He had the weapon in his hand.

DEB. Weapon?

DIANNA. A cricket bat.

> DIANNA *clocks* NASREEN. *She pulls a chair out at the table for* NASREEN.

DEB. A… Right.

> DEB *turns and sees* NASREEN. NASREEN *enters.*

DIANNA. Nasreen. We were worried.

NASREEN. Were you? Why?

DEB. There's this pack of wild animals out on street.

NASREEN. Oh, that. They don't frighten me.

DEB. Scared the shit out of me. Sorry.

NASREEN. I won't allow myself to become a victim.

DIANNA. Good for you.

> STEPHIE *bursts in.*

STEPHIE. Been up and down that bloody… You're here! Aw, thank God. I've been that worried.

She rushes across to hug NASREEN. NASREEN *rebuffs her.* STEPHIE's *a little taken aback.*

Says to 'em, I said, I know I seen her.

NASREEN *turns away from* STEPHIE. STEPHIE *goes across to join* DEB *and* DIANNA *at the table. She sits down. she gives a nervous laugh.*

What are we like, eh? Playing bridge with that lot goin' on out there. What?

NASREEN *stares at* STEPHIE.

What's up?

DEB. Still don't think he done it though.

NASREEN. He had the cricket bat in his hand.

DEB. I never said that. I swear.

DIANNA. I did.

STEPHIE. Why?

DIANNA. Because it's true.

DEB. Don't mean he done it though.

STEPHIE. He's getting help. We're all… Tell her.

NASREEN *takes her glasses and her phone out of her bag and places them on the table. She sits down.*

DEB. You're not stoppin'? Are you?

NASREEN. Well, I'm not going back out there.

DIANNA. Right. Well, we might just as well play then.

NASREEN. Please.

DIANNA. I'll get the cards.

She gets up and fetches the cards. She places them on the table.

DEB. You're dealer.

NASREEN. Thank you.

> NASREEN *deals the cards. They arrange their cards and calculate their hands. A long, long pause as* NASREEN *considers.*

STEPHIE. I never…

DIANNA. Not now.

STEPHIE. No. Sorry.

NASREEN. One spade.

DEB. Pass.

> STEPHIE *takes a little time to consider.*

STEPHIE. Two hearts.

DIANNA. Pass.

> NASREEN *takes a little time to consider.*

NASREEN. Two no trumps.

DEB. Pass.

STEPHIE. Three no trumps.

DIANNA. Pass. So, we're in three no trumps. Deb? You lay the first card.

DEB. Yeah. Hold on.

> *Scrutinising her cards. She lays a card.*

DIANNA. Okay. Dummy?

STEPHIE. Oh, yeah. Right.

> STEPHIE *lays all her cards out on the table.*

NASREEN. Thank you, partner.

DEB (*mimics*). Thank you, partner.

DIANNA. Thank you, Deborah.

DEB. Well, it is a bit daft, int it?

DIANNA. Etiquette.

DEB. Bollocks. Yeah, well it is.

A pause.

STEPHIE. We vulnerable or non-vulnerable?

DEB. Vulnerable.

DIANNA. Don't let's worry about vulnerability for now. Just focus on your hand.

NASREEN's phone goes.

NASREEN. Excuse me, I'll have to get this I'm afraid. I'm on call.

She picks up her phone.

Hello? Where? Okay. Five minutes. Has someone called an ambulance? Okay, fine.

She hangs up.

Someone's been hurt. I'll have to go.

STEPHIE. You're not going back out there?

NASREEN. I'm a doctor. It's what I do.

DEB. Care?

NASREEN. Yes. I'm sorry, I have to go.

She exits.

STEPHIE. D'you think she'll be all right?

DEB *shrugs*.

DIANNA. Of course she will.

STEPHIE *gazes towards the door. Sound of a siren wailing in the distance.*

Scene Five

Several weeks later. On the flip chart in purple ink:
'Intermediate Bridge. Week Three: Reverses and Jump-shifts'.
STEPHIE *is putting baize cloths on the tables. She smoothes the*
cloth with her hands. NASREEN *appears in the doorway.*

STEPHIE. Just setting up.

NASREEN. I'm early.

STEPHIE. Dianna's not here yet.

NASREEN. No. Where's Deb?

STEPHIE. Just run up to Morrisons to get some cigs.

NASREEN. There's a machine in the bar.

STEPHIE. Not her brand.

NASREEN. Okay.

 STEPHIE *picks up her bag and takes out her purse.*

STEPHIE. D'you want a drink? I'm getting one.

NASREEN. No thanks.

STEPHIE. Should be 'ere any minute, the other two.

 Sound of siren wailing in the distance.

NASREEN. Dianna might be late. That's what she said last
 week.

STEPHIE. Did she? Don't remember.

NASREEN. Traffic's very heavy this evening.

STEPHIE. Yeah, I noticed that an' all. Accident most prob'ly.

 NASREEN *gazes at the flip chart.*

Reverses and jump-shifts.

NASREEN. We've come a long way.

STEPHIE. Yeah. Never would of thought I'd of made it.

NASREEN. Dianna's a good teacher.

STEPHIE. She is, yeah. Even Deb thinks so. Her what wanted to learn but... Funny. Don't think I could give it up now.

NASREEN. You're hooked.

STEPHIE. I am, yeah. Like an addiction, int it? The love of the game. Never would of thought it could happen to me.

NASREEN. I feel the same.

A pause.

STEPHIE. She's run out of green ink, look.

NASREEN *laughs.*

NASREEN. She colour-codes. I think. Green for beginners and... That...

STEPHIE. Purple.

NASREEN....For intermediate. So. Reverses and jump-shifts.

STEPHIE. Forcing bids.

NASREEN. Not always.

STEPHIE. No but they can be.

NASREEN. Yes. So many conventions, aren't there?

STEPHIE. There is, yeah.

NASREEN. It's a very tactical game.

STEPHIE. Bit rubbish at all that, me.

NASREEN. You're better than you think.

STEPHIE. Am I? Get me drink.

STEPHIE *heads for the door.*

You sure? [You don't want a drink.]

NASREEN. Yes. Thank you. Stephie?

STEPHIE. What?

NASREEN. No, I just… I just wondered if you'd seen anyone yet?

STEPHIE. I have done, yes.

NASREEN. Is it helpful?

STEPHIE. She's lovely.

NASREEN. Good. Clare, is it?

STEPHIE. D'you know her?

NASREEN. Not personally. But I've heard she's very good. I've referred one or two other people and they've liked her.

STEPHIE. She doesn't do anything. Doesn't say much really. Just gives us time.

NASREEN. To talk?

STEPHIE. If I want. Right, I'll just…

NASREEN. Of course.

> STEPHIE *reaches the door.*

I understand they dropped the case.

> STEPHIE *turns back.*

STEPHIE. Well, they've had to, haven't they?

NASREEN. Insufficient evidence?

> STEPHIE *wanders idly back to the table as she speaks.*

STEPHIE. It were all circumstantial.

NASREEN. He had a cricket bat in his hand.

STEPHIE. Yes. He was playing cricket.

> *She smoothes the cloth with her hands.*

Just get the cards.

> *She goes to the cupboard and takes out the cards.*

NASREEN. So, Jack's word against Mohammed's.

STEPHIE. He never said nothing. Mohammed.

She places the cards on the table.

NASREEN. Can he speak?

STEPHIE. Bidding boxes. 'Scuse me.

She goes back to the cupboard and takes out the bidding boxes.

Spoke to his mother. That's what I've heard. That he's gonna be all right.

NASREEN. No harm done.

STEPHIE. Well, yeah… Obviously, but… They've spoken to 'em. Police. Cautioned 'em.

NASREEN. Good.

Long pause.

And the family therapy…

STEPHIE. It's, yeah… It's helping. I think. Well, it's early days but it's helping me.

NASREEN *nods*.

NASREEN. Good.

STEPHIE. He never done it, Nasreen. I know me own son.

NASREEN. Sometimes we think we know people better than we do.

STEPHIE. Yeah, but… I dunno. She's dead supportive.

NASREEN. Clare?

STEPHIE. Doesn't judge.

NASREEN. She's very professional.

STEPHIE. She likes him, I think.

NASREEN. Jack?

STEPHIE. Folk do.

NASREEN. That little boy could've died.

STEPHIE. I know.

A look from NASREEN.

Been over and over it in me mind.

NASREEN. Did Simon go?

STEPHIE. To family therapy? Jokin' me. Can't see nothing wrong with us.

NASREEN. His son beat a child half to death.

A long pause.

STEPHIE. Not his son, he said. Wouldn't never do a thing like that. Not even to a…

NASREEN. Paki?

STEPHIE. It don't make sense. Simon, right? He's so full of hatred, this… this bile, but even as much as he… Sorry. Even he wouldn't have done a thing like that. Never. Never in a million years he wouldn't. And I can't honestly believe our Jack would either. I'm sorry, I just don't.

NASREEN. This hatred. Where does it come from?

STEPHIE. I've no idea. I swear to God I don't know.

NASREEN. Upbringing maybe.

STEPHIE. Yeah, could be. His dad were same way.

NASREEN. Indoctrination.

STEPHIE. S'pose it is, yeah. And ignorance.

NASREEN. How on earth did you two get together?

STEPHIE. Asked meself that 'nough times. There again, I was only a kid when I met him. You don't think politics at eleven.

NASREEN. I think Mohammed might.

STEPHIE. He… Yeah. Anyhow, it's too late now. I love him. Might feel wrong sometimes but I do.

NASREEN. P'raps it's fear. With Jack.

STEPHIE. What's he got to be frightened of?

NASREEN. The others.

STEPHIE. What others?

NASREEN. It's just that I think sometimes they get themselves into situations they can't handle. Maybe that's what happened.

STEPHIE. I don't know what happened. Well, only what he's told me.

NASREEN. You don't believe him?

STEPHIE. Yes. I do.

A long pause.

He's told her an' all. Clare.

NASREEN. What has he told her?

STEPHIE. The truth.

STEPHIE *looks up at* NASREEN. NASREEN *glances down at* STEPHIE's *wrist.* STEPHIE *tugs her sleeve over her wrist.*

It's not how it looks.

NASREEN. It looks very sore.

STEPHIE. It is. Caught meself on stove.

NASREEN. I believe you.

STEPHIE. No you don't.

NASREEN. If you need somewhere to go…?

STEPHIE. I don't want to leave him. And I don't want to stay.

NASREEN. I'm sorry.

STEPHIE *nods.*

There's always the refuge.

STEPHIE. Refuge?

NASREEN. Somewhere you'll be safe.

STEPHIE. From what? Simon? From me… [husband.] My
God. You just don't get it, do you?

NASREEN. Stephie.

STEPHIE. No, you listen. You listen to me. He never done it.
This –

*She tears her sleeve back and shoves her wrist under
NASREEN's nose.*

I done that. Thinking about you. 'Un all this – (*Beat.*) shit
what's happened. Had I been thinking what I were doing, I
wouldn't never 'ave stuck me hand over flame. So, if you're
looking for someone to blame…

NASREEN. I'm sorry, Stephie, it's just… I'm so worried about
you. I want to be sure you're safe.

STEPHIE. We're none of us safe. Our own worst enemy, aren't
we?

NASREEN. How d'you mean?

STEPHIE. Love. Makes us do daft things.

She looks up at NASREEN.

Like forgiving.

NASREEN. Maybe.

A long pause.

STEPHIE. How's your mum?

NASREEN. Not great.

STEPHIE. You?

NASREEN *shakes her head.*

NASREEN. It feels like drowning.

STEPHIE. I know.

NASREEN *sniffs and blows her nose.*

NASREEN. I help other people. Talk to them. Refer them to counsellors. I'd no idea how it feels.

STEPHIE. It feels like drowning.

STEPHIE *reaches out and takes* NASREEN*'s hand. A long pause.*

Can I get you something? Coffee, tea?

NASREEN *shakes her head.*

J2O?

NASREEN *smiles.*

NASREEN. No thanks.

Screaming siren and a blue light flashes past the window.

Must be an accident.

STEPHIE. Yes. Both of 'em should've been 'ere by now.

NASREEN *glances at her watch.*

NASREEN. Dianna did say she might not get here until about eight o'clock.

STEPHIE. It's half-past gone.

NASREEN. Yes.

STEPHIE. Wonder if Deb's texted me. Can't always hear me phone.

She takes out her phone.

Oh, here we go. Dianna. (*Reading.*) 'Traffic. Miles of it, backed up to...'

Phone rings.

Hello? Oh, hiya yeah, just got your text. Yeah, we did wonder. Where? What round... No, she isn't, not yet. Just went round Morrisons for her cigs. (*Aside to* NASREEN.) Fire. Up near... Eh? Yeah, but there's that old warehouse where the kids hang out, int there? This time last year. Okay then, well, as soon as Deb… She will be, yeah, if it's round her way. Good idea. I could do with the practice. Will do. Bye.

She hangs up and drops the phone back in her bag.

Held up in traffic. There's a fire up round yours. Well, not at yours obviously but round that way. Deb should be back 'ere by now though. Can't think what's keeping her.

DEB *bursts in.*

Talk of the devil… What's up?

DEB. You'll have to come quick. There's a fire at yours.

STEPHIE *and* NASREEN *freeze.*

Your house is on fire, Nasreen. You have to get home. Now!

NASREEN *is still frozen.*

STEPHIE. Are they all right? Sanjay and Sunil. They are all right, Deb? Aren't they?

NASREEN *flies out of the room. Another siren screams past the window, blue lights flashing.*

God. Oh, God. Deb?

DEB. I don't know. I don't know.

Scene Six

The following week. Torrential rain. On the chart in purple ink is, 'Intermediate Bridge. Week Four: Defensive Strategy'. DIANNA *is setting up.* DEB *appears in the doorway.*

DIANNA. Hello there.

DEB. Yeah, hi.

DIANNA. I'm ready if you'd like to come in.

> DEB *glances over her shoulder and enters.*

> What an awful night.

DEB. Wet.

DIANNA. I got soaked just running in from the car. Cloakroom's open if you want to leave that.

DEB. You're all right, thanks. Lost loada gear in past. Cloakrooms. I don't trust 'em.

DIANNA. I'm sure it'd be perfectly safe here.

> DEB *pulls her coat tightly around her.*

DEB. It's designer, me coat.

DIANNA. It suits you.

DEB. Weren't sure it were me. Comfy though. Warm.

DIANNA. You can't sit down in that, you're wet through.

DEB. I'll take it off then.

> *She takes off her coat and puts it over the back of her chair. She takes a newspaper out of her bag.*

> I'll put me paper underneath, look. Save it drippin' on floor. You get your carpets wet 'un they smell rank, don't they? Done it meself 'nough times.

She spreads the paper under the coat.

Walkin'… (*Staring at the paper.*) muck in.

DIANNA. Deb?

DEB. Nothing. Just…

DIANNA. The fire?

DEB. Yeah.

DIANNA. I read it.

DEB. Doesn't say much, though, does it?

DIANNA. Still under investigation.

DEB. Yeah. Well, it would be.

DIANNA. Let's try and focus on our bridge. Hmm?

DEB nods and stands up.

No Stephie this evening?

DEB. Running late.

DIANNA. No problem. Gives us a little time to catch up.

DEB. Why, 'm I behind then?

DIANNA. Not at all, no. In fact, you're all doing so well, I thought we might sign you up for the tournament in the spring.

Brandishes a form.

Hmm?

DEB. No. Thank you. Sooner not.

DIANNA. I've got the forms.

DEB. Yeah. I'm not… Oh.

She roots through her bag and takes out a magazine. She hands it to DIANNA.

Brung you this back.

DIANNA. Was it helpful?

DEB. Never had time.

Wipes her nose on her hand.

DIANNA. Keep it. There are some exercises on bidding towards the front.

DIANNA *begins to flick through the magazine.*

Page four I believe. Here.

DEB. I've no time.

DIANNA. Nasreen won't be here before seven, why don't we...

DEB. She still comin' then?

DIANNA. Yes.

DEB. Right. Don't think I would of.

DIANNA. She did sound a little shaky on the phone.

DEB. She phoned you?

DIANNA. Just to say she was still coming.

DEB. Someone sets fire to your house and you wanna come out and play cards?

DIANNA. Just wants a little time out I think. It can be therapeutic. Thinking about something else.

DEB. S'pose. Yeah, I can see that.

DIANNA (*brandishes magazine*). Let's go over this together.

DEB. No. Just... Sooner we done it for real.

DIANNA. It's good practice.

DEB. No. Thanks. It's not that I don't like reading.

Beat.

DIANNA. I understand.

DEB. Do you?

DIANNA. Yes.

A long pause.

DEB. Seven o'clock gone.

DIANNA. Come and sit down. We can run through defensive strategy.

DEB. You what?

DIANNA. Defending tactics.

DEB. Oh, right. Yeah, why not?

DIANNA. And then maybe vulnerability?

DEB. 'Kay.

DEB draws out a chair and sits down. She wipes her nose on her hand. Sniffs.

They're all right. Her family.

DIANNA. She told me.

DEB. It were just routine. Them taking 'em in.

DIANNA. A precaution.

DEB. Yeah. He doesn't mind her comin' out then? Her husband.

DIANNA. He's very supportive.

DEB. Must be.

DIANNA. I think she needs her bridge at the moment.

DEB nods. She absently toys with her coat.

DEB. Someone at home with the kid?

DIANNA. They're staying at her mother's for a bit.

DEB. She back home then?

DIANNA. Yes.

DEB. Right. Sad.

DIANNA. It is.

DEB. Where is it her mother lives again?

DIANNA. Just up the road from here. Neesdon Park.

DEB. Nice. Would of thought she'd be in the hospital.

DIANNA. She wants to die at home.

DEB. You would do I suppose.

DIANNA. Yes.

DEB. How long's she got?

DIANNA. I don't know. She doesn't really talk about it. Not to me anyway.

DEB. No.

Beat.

DIANNA. They've become quite close, haven't they? Stephie and...

DEB. Hadn't noticed.

DIANNA. ...Nasreen. Funny really.

DEB. Why is it? What, her being working class, you mean?

DIANNA. No, of course not.

DEB. What then?

DIANNA *draws the cards towards her. She starts to shuffle.*

Good area, int it? Neesdon Park.

DIANNA. Very green. Lots of open spaces.

DEB. Not that many up there. Families, you know?

DIANNA. I wouldn't know.

DEB. Yeah, you would. Posh an' all.

DIANNA. Nasreen's your neighbour, isn't she?

DEB. Couple of doors down. I don't see her though. Well, here I do but...

DIANNA. She's very busy.

DEB. I am an' all. Very.

DIANNA. I've forgotten what it is that you do.

DEB. Hairdressing. From home. Not that I need the money now, course, just... I like being busy. Passes time. Not that I'm unhappy. I am. Happy. Got everything I need now, haven't I?

DIANNA *nods*.

Heard engine. Seen it pulling up outside. Siren. Lights. Thought it were ambulance first off. Woman next door's expecting. Weren't amblance though. Fire engine. Couldn't smell nothing in the house but when we got outdoors... This bitter taste in air.

DIANNA. Burning?

DEB. Bitter. 'Un stinging us eyes, you know? Lookin' at our Paul and his eyes are streaming. Makes 'em run, the smoke. Weren't much of a fire but the smoke...

DIANNA. Dreadful.

DEB. I'd say it's that bit safer, Neesdon Park. Because they know these ones what want to attack 'em. They know where they live.

DIANNA. Well, let's hope it doesn't come to that.

DEB. Hope? What bloody good is that, eh?

DIANNA. Deb?

DEB. Sorry. Bit cranky. It's me son.

DIANNA. Has something happened?

DEB. It's no big deal.

DIANNA. Do you want to talk about it?

DEB. No.

A long pause. DIANNA *begins to shuffle the cards.*

He's been done for underage drinking. They all do it. He got caught. I'd a letter in post yes'day morning.

DIANNA. From the police?

DEB. 'Parently, yeah.

DEB *looks away for a moment.*

I'd give the little sod what for but I can't, can I? Not any more. Size of him.

DIANNA. I'm not sure that's the answer.

DEB. What is?

DIANNA *lays the cards back on the table.*

DIANNA. Does he ever talk about his father?

DEB. I'm his mother. He's not gonna talk to me.

DIANNA. It might help.

DEB. He's fourteen.

DIANNA. It must be difficult bringing him up on your own.

DEB. I manage.

DIANNA. He was very young when your husband died.

DEB. Nine. They're selfish, though, aren't they? Kids. Didn't seem that bothered. Not really. Never even cried when I told him. Got up the next morning and he's kicking off because there's no chocolate milk.

DIANNA. And he doesn't...

DEB. Never.

DIANNA. ...talk about his father? How's he getting on at his new school?

DEB. Yeah, fine I think. He doesn't complain.

NASREEN *enters.*

DIANNA. Nasreen.

NASREEN. Hello.

DIANNA. How's things?

NASREEN *gives a little nod and sits down. She takes a*
magazine out of her bag.

NASREEN. This was great, thanks. Luckily, I had it with me at
work.

DIANNA. It's only a magazine.

NASREEN *hands the magazine to* DIANNA.

I'm glad you found it helpful. Did you lose much?

NASREEN. Our dignity.

DIANNA. I don't think so.

DEB. Yeah.

NASREEN *looks at* DEB.

No, what I meant is no. You never.

NASREEN *nods. She looks away for a moment.*

NASREEN. Stephie not coming?

DEB. Running late.

NASREEN. Oh?

DEB. She never said why.

NASREEN. Oh no, fine. I just… I just wondered, that's all.

DEB. She'll be here.

NASREEN. Good.

DEB. I'm sorry. What happened. [About what happened.]
I'm… I'm really sorry for you. Your family an' all. You can
tell 'em from me. You will tell 'em, won't you? Tell 'em I'm
askin' after 'em.

NASREEN. Thanks.

DEB. Can't… Can't imagine, you know.

NASREEN *smiles.*

NASREEN. No one died.

DIANNA. Thank God. You must be devastated, Nasreen. If there's anything at all that I can do...

NASREEN. We'll be fine. Thank you.

DIANNA. Strong family.

NASREEN. Yes.

Long pause.

DEB. Weren't much damage then ?

NASREEN. Cosmetic.

DEB. Good.

DIANNA. Don't underestimate what this has done to you.

NASREEN. No.

DEB. How's littl'un?

NASREEN. He'll be okay.

DIANNA. Nasreen?

NASREEN *shakes her head.*

He's not hurt?

NASREEN. It's the nightmares. I want to... I can't. I can't take it away. The fear.

DIANNA. It'll pass.

DEB. D'you think?

DIANNA. In time.

DEB. Yeah, right.

DIANNA. Do they have any idea who might be involved?

NASREEN. They haven't said. Not yet. But they've found something.

DEB. What?

NASREEN. A phone.

DEB. They'll know then. They must do.

DIANNA. Unless it was destroyed by the fire.

NASREEN. They're not saying. That's all I know. Let's… You know. D'you mind? I just need to think about something else.

DIANNA. Of course.

A pause.

DEB. Has Stephie told you?

NASREEN. What?

DEB. She's stopping at mine.

DIANNA. She's left Simon?

DEB. Not yet.

NASREEN. How is she?

DEB. Up and down.

DIANNA. It's a big step.

NASREEN. Brave.

DEB. Driving my Paul mad 'aving 'em at ours. Does his head in, does Jack.

DIANNA. Really? Why?

DEB. They've never got on, them two.

DIANNA. Pity.

DEB. Plenty of mates, my Paul. Never been short of company.

DIANNA. Jack's pretty popular I believe.

DEB. Yeah, there's one or two.

NASREEN. Quality not quantity.

DEB. How'd you mean?

NASREEN. I'm sorry. Thinking aloud.

DIANNA. How does Jack feel about leaving his dad?

DEB. They've not left him. Not for good anyhow.

NASREEN. You think she'll go back?

DEB. She can't stop at mine for ever.

NASREEN. There's always the refuge.

DEB. He'd never hurt her.

DIANNA. He has hurt her.

NASREEN. Have you seen her wrist?

DEB. She burnt it on stove. She must of said.

NASREEN. She... Yes.

DEB. And what? You didn't believe her?

NASREEN. I wanted to.

DEB. But you didn't. He might be a bit of a bastard sometimes, but he wouldn't hurt a woman.

DIANNA. It's beneath him I suppose.

DEB. You've never even met him.

DIANNA. I don't need to. I know just the sort of man he is.

DEB. No you don't. How can you?

DIANNA. I've met his type before.

DEB. 'His type'? Right. So you'll know how he nursed his own mother through cancer then?

DIANNA. He's a racist thug. He's a...

DEB. No, you listen.

DIANNA. ...racist.

DEB. Them pictures what you see on the news, right? Them children in Africa. Starving. He's got fuck-all to give because they've no money but he's on that phone and donating every fuckin' time. And yeah, he is, he's a racist bastard with a temper on him but that's not all he is. So, no I'm sorry, but you don't. You don't know his *type* at all, lady.

A long pause.

DIANNA. I...

DEB. What?

DIANNA. I apologise.

DEB. For what?

DIANNA. Offending you.

DEB. You 'aven't.

DIANNA. Good.

DEB. Don't give a toss about your views.

A long pause.

NASREEN. They were close, weren't they? Jack and Simon.

DEB. He's not dead.

DIANNA. No, but... No.

DEB. He'll still see him, even if they do split up.

NASREEN. She's a good mother.

DEB. Does her best.

NASREEN. She'll make sure he still sees his father.

DEB. She will do, aye. Got it all planned out. He'll see his dad twice a week and every other weekend. Best of both worlds, if you ask me.

DIANNA. Suits some, I suppose.

DEB. It's not like there's much of a choice really.

STEPHIE *blusters in.*

STEPHIE. Weather.

DIANNA. Dreadful, isn't it?

STEPHIE. Sorry, I'm late. Crisis at home.

NASREEN. Deb's just told us.

DEB. 'Bout Si.

STEPHIE. Nothing much to tell. Bit of a barney. It happens. Well, it does when you've been wed as long as us. Anyway...

NASREEN. Why didn't you tell me?

STEPHIE. 'Bout what?

NASREEN. Stephie.

STEPHIE. I'm stoppin' at hers for a bit, so what? What about you? You all right?

    NASREEN *nods*.

    How about littl'un?

NASREEN. Yes.

STEPHIE. You must be worried sick.

NASREEN. We'll be okay. You need help.

STEPHIE. Me? Don't talk daft.

NASREEN. Nothing's going to change.

STEPHIE. No. Can we drop it? Please.

NASREEN. I'm worried about you.

STEPHIE. Don't be.

NASREEN. Promise me you'll phone. If anything happens, please promise me.

STEPHIE. Nothing's going to happen. I'm at hers.

DEB. You are, yeah. Time being.

STEPHIE. Swear to God, I'll swing for that lad.

DIANNA. Jack?

STEPHIE. That's the third phone he's lost. I said to him, I'm not made of money, Jack. He's borrowed mine for now. I've said to text you when he's ready. He's round a mate's revising. What? That's why I'm late, we've... I'm sorry, love, we've turned the house upside down. I'll tidy up when I get home. What's up? Deb?

NASREEN. The police have found a phone.

STEPHIE. So?

NASREEN. So, is it Jack's?

STEPHIE. No, course it's not Jack's.

NASREEN. You can't be sure.

STEPHIE. Yes, I can.

NASREEN. How?

DEB. Because it's Paul's.

STEPHIE. Say again?

DEB. Because it's Paul's.

STEPHIE. What?

DEB. I'm sorry.

STEPHIE. Sorry!

NASREEN. You didn't know?

STEPHIE. No. I… Jesus. I… Deborah?

NASREEN. But… So, if you didn't know, how could you be so sure?

STEPHIE (*to* DIANNA). Tell her.

DIANNA. I can't confirm Paul's involvement but I can tell you Jack's innocent. He was with me at the time of the fire.

NASREEN. The maths challenge?

DIANNA. Yes.

    STEPHIE *sinks onto a chair.*

    Do the police know?

DEB. Not yet. (*To* NASREEN.) Sorry.

NASREEN. Stephie…

STEPHIE. Yeah, forget it. Just need… Me head. Can't get me head round it.

NASREEN. I can't... [stay.]

DIANNA. No, of course.

STEPHIE. Yeah, just go. God.

NASREEN starts to gather her stuff.

Nasreen, love? I'll call you.

NASREEN. Lovely. Thanks.

She gestures goodbye to DIANNA and exits.

STEPHIE. Can't believe it.

DEB. I've said I'm sorry.

STEPHIE. They could've died. Her whole family just... Wiped out.

DEB. Yeah. I know. I KNOW.

She wipes her nose with her hand.

STEPHIE. And what about... Aw, no, please tell me it wasn't your Paul what done that an' all.

DIANNA. What? Mohammed?

DEB. I didn't... I swear to God, I didn't know till now. But... Think so, yeah.

STEPHIE. Have you heard the names they've been calling my son at school? Have you?

DEB is too overcome to speak.

D'you know what it's like goin' into local shop 'un feeling folk shrinking away? Staring, whispering, calling you stuff under their breath. Or else shouting it out in high street. Gobbing off at us. Or on the bus where there's no place to hide. This woman spat at me the other day. I could taste her saliva on me own tongue. And I don't blame her, not for one minute I don't. Because if someone beat my child half to death, I'd want to do same.

DEB. But, I just... I didn't...

STEPHIE *spits at* DEB.

DIANNA. Stephie!

STEPHIE. What?

She spits again. DEB *breaks down.*

DIANNA. God help us.

DIANNA *sinks onto a chair.* STEPHIE *starts to cry.*

STEPHIE. Why didn't you tell me?

DEB. I was frightened.

STEPHIE. Of what?

DEB. Them takin' him. He's all I've got left. Stephie, please…
Don't… Don't want to be on me own.

A long, long pause, then STEPHIE *goes to* DEB. DEB *falls into her arms.*

I'm sorry, Stephie. I'm so sorry.

STEPHIE. Weren't you what done it.

DEB. I did. I did. It was me.

DIANNA. What?

DEB. I'm responsible for him. S'posed to be.

STEPHIE. He's not a child.

DEB. He's fourteen.

DIANNA. He knows right from wrong, Deborah.

STEPHIE. Yeah.

STEPHIE *moves a stray hair from* DEB*'s face.*

Or he should bloody do.

DEB *nods through her tears.*

DEB. 'Tis, yeah. It's my fault. Brung him up wrong. Not been
there for him. Not… Not been there. I'm so sorry.

STEPHIE. Why though? I mean, why'd he do it?

DEB. Think he misses his dad.

DIANNA. That's no excuse.

DEB. No. There isn't one, is there? Gets in these rages.
Drinking, swearing. Can't do a thing with him. Won't talk to
me. Doesn't wanna know me most the time. P'raps he
blames me.

STEPHIE. What for?

DEB. Rob. I know I blame meself.

STEPHIE. Don't talk daft. Why?

DEB. Me what… Me what phoned him. Havin' a go, like you
do. Where are you? What time are you… Going to be home.
'Un all this. Me what done it. Caused it.

STEPHIE. It were an accident, Deb.

DEB. Yeah, maybe. But this int.

STEPHIE. No.

DIANNA. We should phone the police.

   DIANNA *takes out her phone*.

DEB. No. I will.

STEPHIE (*to* DIANNA). What's going to happen to him?

   DEB *takes out her phone*.

DEB. Prison.

DIANNA. Not for a fourteen-year-old. He might well get a
custodial sentence but he won't go to prison. They have
special places. Secure children's homes.

   DEB *stares at* DIANNA.

STEPHIE. Right. A children's home, Deb. That don't sound too
bad, love.

DEB. Doesn't matter what name you give it.

DIANNA. They'll help him.

DEB. Reform him?

STEPHIE. Make him better.

DEB. Than what?

Beat.

DIANNA. He is.

DEB *looks at* DIANNA *for a moment then nods.*

DEB. Yeah. Thanks.

DIANNA. What for?

DEB. Talkin' to me.

She dials.

Yeah, hi. I want to… I want to talk to someone about me son.

Scene Seven

Some months later. On the noticeboard, details of a charity fun-run, a mothers' day tea, an Easter egg hunt and a jumble sale for the Salvation Army. STEPHIE *and* NASREEN *are hovering beside the noticeboard. On the flip chart scrawled in red ink is: 'Bridge Tournament: Participating Partnerships Please Sign Below'.*

STEPHIE. D'you think?

NASREEN. Why not?

DIANNA *enters.*

DIANNA. Hello.

NASREEN. We're thinking about this.

DIANNA. The tournament?

STEPHIE. Oh, I don't know though.

DIANNA. Go for it. You're more than capable.

DIANNA *hands* STEPHIE *a pen.*

STEPHIE. Go on then. I will.

STEPHIE *adds her name to the list.*

DIANNA. The pair of you?

STEPHIE *looks at* NASREEN. STEPHIE *hands* NASREEN *the pen.*

NASREEN. Yes.

NASREEN *signs her name.* DEB *enters with a pile of magazines.*

DIANNA. Hello, Deb.

DEB. Yeah, hi.

STEPHIE. We've signed up for the tournament.

DEB. You never. Why?

Pause.

STEPHIE. Because I can.

DEB. S'pose.

DIANNA. How about it, Deb?

DEB. No, you're all right, thanks.

DIANNA. Maybe next time.

DEB. Yeah, maybe.

DIANNA (*to* STEPHIE). So. Have you moved in yet?

STEPHIE. Have done, aye. All me stuff's in now. Went round ours for the last thing yes'day morning. This clock me grandma left us. He weren't in. He's doin' all right, Jack says. Cookin', washing, cleaning. Miss him, but…

NASREEN. I know.

DEB. You can always come round ours. Not to live, I don't mean, but… Glass of wine, coffee. Be like old times.

STEPHIE. Thanks, Deb. That'd be nice.

DIANNA. You look a bit laden.

DEB. Just come give 'em you back.

She puts the magazines on the table.

Couldn't give 'em you before.

STEPHIE. Why not?

DEB. Just. You know.

STEPHIE *nods*.

She's gonna help us. Dianna is.

DIANNA. It'll be my pleasure.

STEPHIE. Reading?

DEB. Yeah.

STEPHIE. It's no big deal.

DEB. It is when you can't do it.

NASREEN. Good for you.

    DEB throws NASREEN a look.

    That's…

DEB. What?

    Beat.

NASREEN. Great.

    DEB nods.

DEB. Just him I've gotta work on now. Paul.

STEPHIE. Paul can read.

DEB. Words he can, yeah. It's people he's got a problem with.

STEPHIE. How's he doin'?

DEB. Yeah, he's… You know. Much the same really, bit wild.

DIANNA. Early days.

DEB. 'Tis, yeah. Miss him.

NASREEN. Of course you do.

STEPHIE. Yeah, Deb. You're his mum.

    She gives a wry little laugh.

DEB. I am, God help me. 'Un, d'you know what? He's a knobhead and he's not gonna change overnight but… I do. I love him.

    NASREEN smiles.

NASREEN. A strong family.

    DEB stares at NASREEN.

DEB. Yeah. Maybe.

    NASREEN holds her gaze.

    The End.

A Nick Hern Book

Pack first published in Great Britain in 2012 as a paperback original by Nick Hern Books Limited, The Glasshouse, 49a Goldhawk Road, London W12 8QP, in association with Papatango and the Finborough Theatre

Cover image: www.shutterstock.com
Cover design: Ned Hoste, 2H

Typeset by Nick Hern Books, London
Printed in Great Britain by Mimeo Ltd, Huntingdon, Cambridgeshire PE29 6XX

A CIP catalogue record for this book is available from the British Library

ISBN   978 1 84842 306 0

www.nickhernbooks.co.uk

 facebook.com/nickhernbooks

 twitter.com/nickhernbooks